Deception in Dickens' *Little Dorrit*

American University Studies

Series IV
English Language and Literature

Vol. 80

PETER LANG
New York • Bern • Frankfurt am Main • Paris

Library of Congress Cataloging-in-Publication Data

Rotkin, Charlotte
    Deception in Dickens' Little Dorrit / Charlotte
Rotkin.
        p. cm. — (American university studies. Series IV,
English language and literature ; vol. 80)
        Bibliography : p.
        1. Dickens, Charles, 1812-1870.   Little Dorrit.
2. Deception in literature.   I. Title.   II. Series.
PR4562.R68   1989   823'.8 — dc19   88-12080
ISBN 0-8204-0721-6   CIP
ISSN 0741-0700

CIP-Titelaufnahme der Deutschen Bibliothek

Rotkin, Charlotte:
Deception in Dickens' Little Dorrit / Charlotte
Rotkin. — New York; Bern; Frankfurt am Main;
Paris: Lang, 1989.
    (American University Studies: Ser. 4, English
    Language and Literature; Vol. 80)
    ISBN 0-8204-0721-6

NE: American University Studies / 04

© Peter Lang Publishing, Inc., New York 1989

Printed by Weihert-Druck GmbH, Darmstadt, West Germany

Charlotte Rotkin

Deception in Dickens'
Little Dorrit

PETER LANG
New York • Bern • Frankfurt am Main • Paris

For my Father
And my Husband

Contents

Note on References and Editions

I am using the Penguin English Library Edition of Charles Dickens' *Little Dorrit*, which follows other major texts in that it is based on the Charles Dickens Edition of 1868, which was revised by Dickens himself. Differences in the 1868 edition from the original serial publication of December 1855–June 1857, consist mainly of alterations in punctuation. One of the changes appears in the name of Mr. F.'s Aunt: the original serial publication shows "aunt" in lower case; the 1868 revised edition alters the noun to upper case. This change suggests Dickens' reconsideration of the importance of the Aunt's role in the novel.

Quotations from *Little Dorrit* in the text of my study are followed by a chapter number, in Arabic numerals, within parentheses. The abbreviations used in the notes follow the titles of the additional Penguin Editions used in the text.

Little Dorrit: L D
Nicholas Nickleby: NN
Martin Chuzzlewit: MC
David Copperfield: D C
Great Expectations: G E

Introduction

In *Novels and Novelists*, Dickens is described by his contemporary, John Cordy Jeaffreson, as:

> deceitful, deceiving, and wittingly dishonest a describer as can be found in the entire range of living authors. The triumph of his art is the perfection of his deceit. . . . Clennam is nothing as the book goes but a good man,—that is less than the nineth part of one.

Although Jeaffreson evaluates the hero of *Little Dorrit* with penetrating insight, he does not elaborate on Dickens' narrative strategy or on his character analysis. It is the task, therefore, of this study to expand on Jeaffreson's commentary and to show the manner and method of Dickens' devious strategies in *Little Dorrit*.

It has frequently been observed that *Little Dorrit* is a novel about spiritual and physical imprisonment. What has not been sufficiently recognized is that, in addition, *Little Dorrit* is a novel about deception. It is the central argument of this book that *Little Dorrit* is a deceptive presentation of deception. It deludes the reader with false images of its most significant characters. It overwhelms the reader with stimuli in order to hide the ambiguities which undermine the false images of characterization. It misleads the reader by presenting, but not quite approving, Victorian standards of morality. Virtue, a common gauge for a Victorian heroine, is ambiguously presented in the portrait of Amy Dorrit. Although the major characters (and some of the subsidiary ones) are deceptively portrayed, not all of the characters in *Little Dorrit* are misleading. A close reading of the work shows that Dickens intention-

ally reserves his equivocal representations for the most important characters in this novel.

Many of the secondary characters in *Little Dorrit* are straight-
forwardly presented; others are drawn with "broad satiric
strokes." In *Aspects of the Novel* (1927), E. M. Forster makes the
general observation that Dickens' use of broad satire enhances
recognition of his characters. Forster's comments are applicable
to most of the characters in *Little Dorrit*. They are clearly what
their images signify. They are delineated in detail to reveal their
good or bad qualities, but there are no hidden features to their
personalities. They are human types who are readily discernible. The easily recognized traits of hypocrisy, pretentiousness,
pride and villainy with which the book is concerned, are
presented forthrightly or satirically so that the reader can
immediately classify the person represented. However, Dickens' interest in depth of character is centered primarily on six
individuals selected from a large cast. The complex portraits
found in Amy, Arthur, Fanny, Mrs. Clennam, Flora and Mr.
F.'s Aunt have not been adequately analyzed, and therefore
require clarification.

These six characters are unerring psychological delineations
which depict various hidden forces that motivate their actions.
They incorporate the paradoxes and ambiguities of human
behavior and are deceptive in the image they project.[1] The
reason that they have not been recognized as deceptive char-
acterizations and therefore have not been adequately analyzed
is due to Dickens' inconsistent technique of portraying his cast.
He presents most of them unambiguously, but the six already
mentioned are rendered with cunning ambiguity. If everyone
in the novel were deceptively drawn it would be easier for the
reader to discover the secret of Dickens' narrative strategy. But
because only the most important personages are deviously
portrayed, the reader tends to regard these six portraits as
being as obvious as most of the others. The inclusion of a few
deceitfully drawn characters is part of Dickens' misleading
narrative strategy. The large cast functions as a kind of misdirection away from the few, providing abundant stimuli to

absorb the reader's attention and misdirect him from the subtleties and ironies delicately portrayed in the most important characters. The equivocal nature of characterization in these six individuals assures that *Little Dorrit* will not be fully understood by most of Dickens' audience.

In the narrow focus of this book, I have ignored many themes, characters and subjects to which other critics have rewardingly directed their energies. My specialized approach has enabled me to execute a minute dissection of these six significant characters, which expands awareness of Dickens' eleventh novel and offers an interpretation for consideration that challenges the bias of countless critics who continue to misperceive hero and heroine in terms of an implausible piety. It is my hope that by the broadly based psychological explication of the central characters' language and behavior that this study provides, a new direction of appreciation for the intricacies and gradations of deceit in *Little Dorrit* will be available to readers of Victorian literature in general and to Dickensians in particular. The current trend in psychological criticism and the recent scholarship addressing Dickens' psychological acumen mark my approach a timely one.

Specialists in nineteenth century criticism may conceivably and correctly argue that subterfuge is a Dickensian hallmark, but their argument focuses on the superficial elements in Dickens' fiction. My book addresses the intrinsic properties of Dickens' deceptive techniques. In addition, it traces the values Dickens allots to differing degrees and forms of deception, some of which he acknowledges to be necessary and harmless; others he perceives to be injurious to personal development, and still others he regards as detrimental to the public welfare.

Although the theme of deception is present in various forms in other Dickens novels, the manifestation of deceit is not dealt with in precisely the same way that it is treated in *Little Dorrit*. For example, Dickens incorporates deception in *Great Expectations*. The reader is misled into believing that Miss Havisham is Pip's benefactor, and doesn't learn the truth until the end of the novel. The hero and reader make the discovery simultaneously that Abel Magwitch is Pip's patron. However the misdirection here does not center on an ambiguous portrayal of character, but on plot contrivance. The narrator, who is in possession of the secret, does not share the information with either Pip or the reader. In addition, the self-delusion of the protagonists functions differently in the two novels. Although Pip deludes himself, as a young adult, into believing that he is a gentleman, he does not defraud the reader by his arrogance. However, Amy misleads herself and many readers into believing that she is the personification of virtue.

David Copperfield presents another example of Dickens' treatment of deception. In the earlier novel the reader is taken into the author's confidence, and knows when the characters are dissembling. Even though the hero is misled, the reader is not. Part of Dickens' narrative strategy in *David Copperfield* is to inform the audience of dissimulation through the voices of the narrator and of other characters. The reader is, in effect, privileged to share information which the youthful hero is incapable of absorbing, until the latter eventually acknowledges what the reader has known all along—that he must learn to control his "undisciplined heart." Whereas David deceives himself about Steerforth's friendship, and Amy deludes herself about Dorrit's love, the self-delusion of the protagonists in *David Copperfield* and in *Great Expectations* is dissimilar to that presented in *Little Dorrit*. Ultimately, David becomes aware of Steerforth's selfishness, but Amy can never fully acknowledge Dorrit's egotism. *David Copperfield* maintains a vision of the world in which hope can yet prevail; *Little Dorrit* offers a view of life that is considerably less sanguine. Dickens indicates in the latter work that a paucity of faith is a concomitant of a world devoid of individual transformation.

Based in part on his darkening vision in *Little Dorrit*, Dickens is cautious about overtly taking the audience into his confidence. The reader must approach this grim novel without preconceptions regarding Victorian heroes and heroines. The modern reader needs to disavow Forster's prejudicial view of Dickens' characters as caricature, and to look beneath the surface of characterization if he is to perceive the conflicting and contradictory emotions which motivate the behavior of the Dorrit, Clennam and Casby families. These representations incorporate certain paradoxes and equivocations in characterization not found in *David Copperfield* or *Great Expectations*, and are particularizations of the subtle and pervasive theme of deceit which infuses *Little Dorrit*.

Notes

[1] See Brian Rosenberg on the difficulty of disentangling style from substance and discerning virtue from evil in "The Language of Doubt in *Oliver Twist*," in *Dickens Quarterly*, (June 1987), 98.

1

Criticism: A Developing Awareness of the Complexity of Little Dorrit

This chapter confronts some of the representative criticism of *Little Dorrit* from 1855 to the present. By considering the criticism in this fashion, in a separate chapter, I have been able to concentrate the attributions in one section and to eliminate endnotes almost entirely in the following chapters. The reason for the limited number of notes in subsequent chapters is due to my new interpretation of the role that deception and hostility play in *Little Dorrit*, especially in interactions between the characters. Although unconventional in design, it seems to me a useful technique, since my analyses of these themes in succeeding chapters are, so far as I can determine, critically original. Insofar as the focus of this text departs from traditional interpretations of the hero and heroine in *Little Dorrit*, a somewhat similar departure in design appears felicitous in terms of the unity of this book.

Contemporary and modern critical responses to *Little Dorrit* vary in recognizing the profundity of Dickens' art. Whereas mid- and late twentieth century critics have greatly expanded our understanding of Dickens' artistry, neither contemporary nor the preceding modern criticism has penetrated into some of the ambiguities of characterization in *Little Dorrit*. Insufficient recognition has been accorded to the intricate delineation of character in Dickens' eleventh novel. Attention to the opposing impulses which motivate the actions and behavior of Amy, Arthur, Flora, and Mrs. Clennam has been inadequate. It is a commonplace that Amy is dutiful, Arthur obtuse, Flora inappropriate and Mrs. Clennam undemonstrative. But other equally important traits in these characters have gone unremarked. Amy's hostility has been ignored. Arthur's perversity has gone unnoticed. Flora's pain has been unacknowledged. And Mrs. Clennam's yearning has eluded comment.

More surprising than inadequacies in interpretation are the errors made by eminent commentators in confounding characters and misreading plot. In *Appreciations and Criticisms of the Works of Charles Dickens* (1911), G. K. Chesterton confuses a minor and a major character in *Little Dorrit*. He substitutes the wayward son, Edward (Tip) Dorrit, for the central figure of the father, William Dorrit. Describing the victory of hapless events over a soul, Chesterton writes: "The circumstances are the financial ruin and long imprisonment of Edward Dorrit; the soul is Edward Dorrit himself."[1] It is around William's incarceration that the story revolves; not Edward's. Edward is the heroine's indolent brother whose importance to the tale is subsidiary.

In *Charles Dickens: His Life and Work* (1934), Stephen Leacock arrives at an identical confusion of these two characters. Leacock writes: "Nor is there any more marvelous depiction in all fiction than that of Edward Dorrit."[2] Like Chesterton, Leacock fails to distinguish between Edward the son and William the father.

Another instance of character misidentification occurs in *Dickens' Use of Women in His Novels* (1967), by Sylvia Jarmuth. She writes: "Little Dorrit sustains her grandfather's spirits and saves him from crime." Jarmuth has not only confused two characters, she has confounded two of Dickens' novels. Little Dorrit has no grandfather; the character to whom Jarmuth is referring is Little Nell, heroine of *The Old Curiosity Shop*, who comforts her dispirited grandfather and discourages his criminal activity by resorting to a clever ruse.

Critical errors regarding plot situations in *Little Dorrit* are made by Sylvere Monod, Angus Wilson, and William Burgan. In *Dickens the Novelist* (1968), Monod states that Mrs. Clennam leaves her house "in order to visit her son in prison." Monod errs. Mrs. Clennam does leave her house, but she does not visit her incarcerated son. She pays a call on Amy in order to exact a promise from Little Dorrit that she will never (during Mrs. Clennam's lifetime) reveal the fact that Mrs. Clennam has withheld a legacy from her (II, 31, 858).

In the article, "Dickens on Childhood and Children" (1970), Angus Wilson makes reference to the romance *Paul and Virginia*, saying that it was the "book which Flora had borrowed from Arthur in 'those foolish far off days.' "[3] Wilson mistakes the transaction. It is Arthur who has borrowed the book from Flora and returned it "without note or comment" (I, 13, 195), a fact that causes Flora great distress.

In his article "People in the Setting of *Little Dorrit*" (1973), William Burgan mistakes the house at which Little Dorrit knocks. He claims it is Maggy's house. That is not so. It is a stranger's house. Little Dorrit does not specify the house as Maggy's; instead, she falsely suggests it as a temporary lodging for the poor grotesque (I, 14, 216).

In addition to errors in scholarship, the critical canon reveals a history of inadequate readings of *Little Dorrit*. Many (although not all) early critics regarded *Little Dorrit* as lacking in style, characterization, and power. Insensitivity to Dickens' narrative strategies in *Little Dorrit* are not difficult to find in the nineteenth century. In *The Saturday Review* (1857), Fitzjames Stephen discusses the artistic demerits of *Little Dorrit*. Stephen observes that the story is structurally unsound, having no beginning, middle or end, and that the tale lacks taste. He goes on to state that "It is the cultus of the middle class to purchase Dickens; but an Act of Parliament would fail to enforce the serious reading of [*Little Dorrit*]."[4] In *The Westminster Review* (1856) George Eliot writes:

> We have one great novelist who is gifted with the utmost power of rendering the external traits of our town population; and if he could give us their psychological character . . . with the same truth as their idioms and manners, his books would be the greatest contribution Art has ever made to the awakening of social sympathies. But while he can

copy Mrs. Plornish's colloquial style . . . he scarcely ever passes from
the humorous and external to the emotional and tragic.[5]

In *Fraser's Magazine* (1857), William Forsyth writes that Dickens'
"later works have proceeded in a descending scale. That which
is now issuing from the press, *Little Dorrit*, is decidedly the
worst. His tone is melodramatic throughout." In *Blackwood's
Magazine* for the same year, Edward B. Hamley writes: "we
can't wait for the end of the wilderness of *Little Dorrit* before
recording our earnest protest and deep lament; for in that
wilderness we sit down and weep for thee, O *Pickwick!*"

Not all nineteenth-century criticism of *Little Dorrit* is negative. When the first monthly issue appeared in December 1855,
The Athenaeum heralded its appearance. The reviewer writes
that "here is the commencement of a racy and vigorous tale, a
canvas crowded with original and interesting people." At the
conclusion of the serialization in June 1857, *The Athenaeum*
reported on *Little Dorrit* again. The anticipatory delight which
marked the original critique is repeated and expanded upon in
an analysis which comments perceptively on Dickens' characterization and style. Referring to the realistic portrait of Mrs.
Clennam, the brilliant invention of the Circumlocution Office,
and the vivid description of the Marshalsea, William Hepworth
Dixon writes: "There is enough genius in this book to have
made a sensation for any other name."

Although contemporary critics did not unanimously acclaim
Little Dorrit, Dickens never lost his popular appeal. Authorities
recording early sales of *Little Dorrit* differ in their statistics, but
even the lowest estimate is impressive. In *Dickens: The Critical
Heritage* (1971), Collins states that 36,000 copies of the first
edition of *Little Dorrit* were sold, whereas in *Charles Dickens and
His Publishers* (1978), Patten claims that 63,000 copies were
sold.[6] Even the discrepant figures indicate a wide popular
appeal for the novel.

Although Dickens remained popular with the public
throughout his lifetime, many of the early critics misread and
misunderstood his later works. Much of the adverse criticism

directed against Dickens by his contemporaries contains qualifying statements about him as a deficient genius. In 1856 Hippolyte Taine acknowledges in his essay "Charles Dickens: son talent et ses oeuvres" that Dickens has a "potent style" but argues that his poetic imagination is close to madness. Taine observes that Dickens lacks a sense of beauty and harmony which deprives him of sublimity. Opposing Taine's view, John Cordy Jeaffreson writes in *Novels and Novelists* (1858) that Dickens is a great poet and that his novels are the "prose-poems" of the times.[7] Nevertheless, Taine's critique of Dickens' deficient talent is echoed into the eighties by such commentators as Bagehot, Whipple, Lewes and Morris. An article which Collins attributes to Walter Bagehot appeared anonymously in 1858 in *The National Review*. Bagehot, reflecting Taine's critique, writes that Mr. Dickens' "genius is essentially irregular and unsymmetrical." Edwin Whipple, missing Dickens' psychological nuances, claims in *Atlantic Monthly* (1864) that "the characters in *Little Dorrit* are 'hit off' rather than delineated." In *The Fortnightly Review* (1872), George Henry Lewes snobbishly attributes what he considers to be Dickens' vulgarity to a lack of a classical education. He cannot understand why so ill-educated a writer can have such a vast public appeal. Echoing Lewes on Dickens' meager education, Mobray Morris writes in *The Fortnightly Review* (1882), that Dickens' "prime defect, the defect from which all his others spring" is the want of a classical education.

At the turn of the century, Andrew Lang attacks *Little Dorrit* for its lack of unity. In his Introduction to the Gads Hill edition of *Little Dorrit* (1897), Lang claims that it is not a good book because "the threads of combined narrative are not skillfully interwoven."[8] In his misinterpretation of the book's unified structure, Lang is supported in 1934 by Stephen Leacock. Leacock judges the structure to be unwieldly. In *Charles Dickens: His Life and Work*, Leacock writes: "The parts do not come together as natural components of a common climax." But appreciation of the unified structure of *Little Dorrit* is a theme to which much attention has been devoted in the mid- and later twentieth century. In a penetrating study, Edmund Wilson observes in "Dickens: The Two Scrooges" (1940), that the symbol of immurement which pervades the novel is manifest not only by the presence of the Marshalsea, but it is apparent in the characters who are incarcerated by "imprisoning states of mind." An important study examines the motif of unity in *Little Dorrit*. In *Charles Dickens: The World of His Novels* (1958) J. Hillis Miller observes that "No other of [Dickens'] novels has such a somber unity of tone."[9] And in "*Little Dorrit*: A World in Reverse" (1970), Richard Stang goes further in critical appreciation of *Little Dorrit* in his perceptive analysis of the way in which the component parts of the novel cohere to create a unified structure. Stang argues that *Little Dorrit* is "one of the best integrated [of Dickens' novels] to which almost every chapter, almost every scene, almost every image, make a significant contribution." More than a decade afterwards, Smith draws our attention to *Little Dorrit* as "the one novel in which Dickens attains aesthetic and abstract unity."[10]

Recent criticism owes a debt to Edmund Wilson's pioneering essay which paved the way for future psychological and symbolic interpretations of Dickens' work. In 1939, Wilson inaugurated a series of lectures at the University of Chicago in which he engaged in a reassessment of Dickens' art.[11] This turning point in Dickensian criticism was subsequently published in Wilson's brilliant essay, "Dickens: The Two Scrooges" which marked the beginning of modern Dickens criticism. Aware of Dickens' use of psychology, symbolism, and of his bitter disillusionment with the world (shown particularly in his later novels) Wilson expanded the scope of critical analysis by his recognition of Dickens' depth and complexity. In discussing Dickens' treatment of individual psychology, Wilson notes that it had taken a "distinctly new" turn.[12] Wilson correctly argues that the character of William Dorrit, as a man on whom prison has affected profound psychic changes, is a more thoughtful and penetrating study than any which had preceded it. Dorrit, an amiable and shy man when he enters the Marshalsea, evolves into a vain, proud and selfish character during his incarceration.[13] Prison in *Little Dorrit* is being used by Dickens as more than a social symbol; it is a subjective symbol of dehumanization which perverts Dorrit's personality.

In addition to Wilson's pioneering insights into Dickens' use of psychology, recent criticism is indebted to George Orwell for his awareness of Dickens' concern with human nature, although Orwell is not as perceptive of Dickens' symbolism as is Wilson. Orwell's essay on Dickens, which pays tribute to the novelist as a moral writer, appeared almost simultaneously with Wilson's lectures on the novelist. But Orwell, unlike Wilson, preferred the Pickwickian Dickens to the dark Dickens. In *Dickens, Dali & Others* (1946) Orwell writes that it is a pity that Dickens "deserted the vein of Pickwick for things like *Little Dorrit* and *Hard Times.*" Although Orwell discerningly assesses Dickens' target as being "not so much society as 'human nature,' " he is unable to link Dickens' ability to criticize human nature with his ability to analyze human nature. Unresponsive to Dickens' superb characterization, except as caricature which endures, Orwell is additionally critical of Dickens' unscientific mind. The reader, writes Orwell, is never told what Doyce's invention is.

It is true that it would be of interest to know what the invention is, but Orwell misses the symbolic function of Doyce's appearance in the novel. The inventor's purpose, as Leavis notes, is that Doyce represents Dickens' "positive conception of the artist and of art." Doyce symbolizes the concept of the creative mind as daring and original in thought, disciplined and exact in carrying out his ideas. Dickens describes him as "one of the chosen" (II, 22, 735). His engineering invention has taken many years of his life to perfect and has been subject to many more years of rejection from the Circumlocution Office (I, 10, 160–1). Yet Doyce is tenacious in his belief that his work is meritorious. Clennam observes him, many years after completion of the invention, looking over the models and drawings and consoling himself "that the thing was as true as it ever was" (II, 8, 569). Doyce's faith in himself and in his ingenuity ultimately places him beyond the destruc-

tive reach of governmental agencies, such as the Circumlocution Office. Although the Circumlocution Office denies him a
patent for his invention, his tenacity, patience and faith in his
creativity are finally rewarded. France values his artistry and
ingenuity. His invention is patented on the continent and his
talent is corroborated. For Dickens, creativity triumphs.

In direct antithesis to Orwell's view that Dickens knows
nothing about Doyce's job, and in general knows nothing
about his characters' occupations, Humphry House (1941)
offers a more precise judgment of Dickens' recognition of the
role that work plays in his characters' lives. House states:
"Nearly everyone in Dickens has a job: there is a passionate
interest in what people do for a living and how they make
do."[14] For Dickens, a character's speech is infused with his
occupation. Even William Dorrit, who has no occupation,
creates one for himself while he remains in the Marshalsea, and
his speech mirrors the ironically lofty position he has drafted
for himself as Father of the Marshalsea. He guards his status as
though he received a fixed remuneration from his position.
Ironically he creates an income from mendicancy by his insistence on "testimonials" which accrue to him precisely because
he has made an occupation for himself in becoming the Father
of the Marshalsea. "Testimonials" are frequently the subject of
his discourse.

House notes that metaphors from money: "payment, debt,
return—are abnormally common in Dickens' moral language."
Randolph Splitter observes that money is a recurrent theme in
Little Dorrit engaging all strata of society from the impoverished
in Bleeding Heart Yard to the wealthy in Cavendish Square.[15]
Money functions on all levels in *Little Dorrit* as one of the
manifestations of the novel's overriding theme of imprisonment. The theme of psychological imprisonment inherent in
Little Dorrit is the focus of Splitter's essay. Splitter argues that
the strength of *Little Dorrit* is based on Dickens' obsessive
recollection of the blacking factory trauma which led him to an
entire social vision. Splitter accepts the judgment of many
critics, a view initiated by Wilson and supported by Johnson,

who regard the three-month incident at Warren's as crucial in Dickens' life.

What makes Splitter's analysis incomplete is that it ignores earlier and equally traumatic circumstances in Dickens' life, events to which Hutter quite properly attends. Hutter's awareness of the additional emotional problems in young Charles' life provides a modern, comprehensive portrait of Dickens as a boy. Hutter's "Reconstructive Autobiography" (1977), modifies the Wilson-Johnson-Splitter approach and convincingly argues that other experiences during Dickens' formative years exerted an equally forceful impression on Dickens as did the blacking factory episode. Hutter points to the sibling rivalry Dickens felt toward his sister Fanny, an attitude of envy and competition, which Victorian culture did not acknowledge. The culture denied to young Charles natural feelings of enviousness he felt toward Fanny's success. When Charles was ten years old, two years before he was sent to the blacking factory, Fanny won a music scholarship. She was therefore able to extend her education at approximately the same time that Dickens had to curtail his studies. Victorian culture, writes Hutter, "denies the normalcy of envy and aggression and reinforces Dickens' own overwhelming need to make himself helpless and pitiable as he remembers this episode."[16]

The memory of himself as "pitiable and helpless" was compounded for Dickens two years later, by the frustrating rage he felt at his parents for forcing him into drudgery at Warren's.[17] What remained of these unresolved feelings of envy and aggression toward sister and parents were transferred to a more culturally acceptable anger directed against the blacking factory. The memory of Warren's was not solely the remembrance of an edifice situated at Hungerford Stairs. It became a symbol of catastrophic fate in terms of Dickens' sense of loss, humiliation, marginality and hunger. The name of the locale itself, Hungerford Stairs, conjures deprivation. To have had hateful feelings toward a mercantile organization would have been easier for Dickens to cope with than to recall, and in the recollection, to relive, the intensity of his rancorous feelings

toward parents and siblings. Yet there exists a further compli-
cation in the sibling relationship which Hutter neglects to
mention. This is the problem of Charles' perception of abandonment by Fanny. Harry Stone's "The Love Pattern in Dickens' Novels" (1970), elucidates this point to provide a more
complete picture of the trauma in Charles' early life. Stone
notes that Fanny served as Dickens' surrogate mother while he
was an infant. Sister and brother were inseparable as children.
The period of their closeness began when Dickens was two
years old and his mother, Elizabeth Barrow Dickens, transferred her primary attentions from Charles to the next born
sibling, "a turning away which was compounded in the following years by a steady procession of new brothers and
sisters. Dickens never got over this early turning away."

When Fanny's attention was withdrawn from Charles, after
some eight years of devotion, Dickens felt a second abandonment of female love. The dissolution of their close relationship
occurred two years before the blacking factory incident. When
in 1822 the family abruptly moved from Chatham to London,
Fanny moved out of the Dickens' household shortly thereafter
to accept her scholarship as a pupil-boarder to the Royal
Academy of Music.[18] The envy Charles felt at Fanny's success
was compounded by his sense of loss. He was being deprived
of his sister's loving presence and of his education. Moreover,
these childhood crises did not abate. At twelve, instead of
resuming his formal education, Charles was sent to work at
Warren's. Almost immediately another catastrophic event occurred in the young boy's life. Eleven days after Charles began
work in the blacking factory, his father was arrested for debt.
The rest of the family, except for young Charles, moved into
the Marshalsea Debtor's Prison.

Each of these events, occurring within a relatively short time
span, must have had a cumulative effect on the young boy. In
all likelihood he would have experienced a tremendous sense
of loss. The two most difficult deprivations were the separa-
tions, first from Fanny, and second from his parents. In infancy
Charles had felt abandoned by his mother; subsequently not

only did his sister forsake him, but his mother deserted him a second time. This pattern of repudiation by females was to be repeated when, in 1833, Charles was spurned by his sweetheart Maria Beadnell, a rejection which was followed four years later by what Charles must have construed as the ultimate abandonment, the death of his beloved sister-in-law, Mary Hogarth.

Stone links these thwarted love relationships in Dickens' life to his art and to his choice of a mate. Stone convincingly argues that Dickens yearned for a composite mother-sister-first love in a marriage partner which was impossible of attainment. But Stone is less persuasive when he extends his theory to *Little Dorrit*, declaring that Amy exemplifies this complex notion. He states that the "brother-sister quality in the love relationship between hero and heroine acts as a barrier or deterrent to sexual love and fulfillment."

The love relationship in *Little Dorrit* fulfills a different need from that of a brother-sister. It would be more accurate to describe it as an attempted realization of a libidinal impulse. Arthur Washburn Brown quite properly reminds us in *Dickens' Props* (1967) that Amy achieves some sort of transferred sexual union with her father through marriage to Arthur. Arthur takes her father's place in the same cell in the Marshalsea. He is served by Amy in the same manner and in the identical clothing she wore when attending to William. Amy's transferred sexual union occurs when Arthur's "figure has fused as much as it possibly can with that of Mr. Dorrit."[19] Clennam functions as a surrogate father to Amy and she a surrogate child-mother to him, thereby instilling a subtle incestuous quality to the relationship.[20] When Amy thinks of Arthur she muses on what a good father he would be (I, 14, 210), and when she writes to him she signs herself "your poor child" (II, 14, 524). Attending to Arthur in the old room in the Marshalsea, Amy nurses him as "lovingly . . . as she had nursed her father in that room" (II, 29, 825). When Arthur thinks of Amy he perceives her as if she were a child (I, 9, 136), until he eventually comes to understand that Amy is "the centre of the interest in his life . . . the termination of everything . . . good and pleasant in it" (II, 27, 801–2). For Arthur, Little Dorrit is not only a child, she is the spontaneously loving and gentle mother he never had. She functions not as a mother-sister to Arthur (the role to which Stone assigns her) but rather as a child-mother to him. In addition she cannot exemplify a first love to Arthur since Flora preceded Little Dorrit in Arthur's affections.

Although Stone misreads the love relationship in *Little Dorrit*, he presents an interesting hypothesis regarding the ideal wife Dickens sought. An analysis of Dickens' correspondence to Catherine suggests that, although Dickens may have been seeking such a mate, he was unsuccessful in establishing a relationship that could even approach the ideal. In *Mr. and Mrs. Charles Dickens: His Letters to Her* (1972), edited by Walter Dexter, Dexter presents a chronology of correspondence from the time of Dickens' courtship of Kate to a period of some ten years after their separation. Surprisingly, Dexter does not interpret either the letters or their significance in terms of their revelations about both Charles and Catherine. Neither does Dexter point to any of the patterns in their relationship which emerge from the correspondence. However, in a recent study, *Dickens and Women* (1983), Michael Slater writes rewardingly on Dickens as man and artist partially through his interpretation of Dickens' letters to his wife. Citing that correspondence, Slater perceptively suggests, among numerous other fresh insights, that Dickens had a strong capacity for personal self-delusion. In addition, Slater convincingly argues for a more psychologically complex analysis of Dickens' art and emotional history, than previous biographers have brought forward. Unearthing new material, Slater sees evidence of Dickens' own aggression surfacing in various character portrayals, particularly with his patterning of the infamous Quilp.

One of the patterns which surfaces in Dickens' letters to Kate reveals her predisposition to jealousy, and Dickens' predilection for denial. In a written message dated December 18, 1835, posted from White Hart, Kettering, where Dickens is reporting on an election, he writes:

I perceive you have not yet subdued one part of your disposition, your distrustful feelings and want of confidence. However this may be, you may rest satisfied that I love you dearly—far too well to feel hurt by what in anyone else would have annoyed me greatly.

Apparently the problem of Kate's distrust is not a new one, and although Dickens denies that she has hurt his feelings, the ambiguity of his last sentence indicates otherwise. If he had not been pained by her mistrust he would have no need to deny it. No offense would have been mentioned. Similarly, if he had not been irritated to some degree he would not have found it necessary to indicate that a want of confidence expressed by anyone else would have vexed him greatly.

In another letter during the same year there is a pleading tone to Dickens' reply to his wife. The inference from his response is that Kate has accused him of neglecting her. He implores her to refrain from saying that she is angry at hearing from him and declaring that he "could come to her if [he] would."[21] These early letters reiterate the themes of accusation, recrimination and conciliation, raising the problematic question of why Dickens continued to woo her and, finally, to wed her.

In addition to his love for Kate, there are quite possibly psychological impulses impelling his pursuit of her. He may have continued to court her because he didn't want a repetition of the pattern of loss he had experienced with his mother, Fanny and Maria. The loss of still another woman's love (Catherine's) might have proved too painful. Fear of losing Kate might explain his pleading with her not to be angry with him. Yet paradoxically he may have accepted Kate's negative traits because he was subconsciously repeating a pattern of negative ineraction with a female, a mode of negativism established by his feelings in regard to his mother. In any event, Dickens was aware of Catherine's dissatisfactions with their relationship and her defects (if such they were) long before their marriage. In fact what Dickens was doing in his pursuit of Catherine was committing himself to a relationship in which it was evident that there would continue to be enduring areas of friction about which, in later life, Dickens would come to feel "pitiable and helpless."

Another pattern relating to Kate's mistrust emerges from the letters. This motif establishes Dickens' injudicious manner of communicating with his wife on certain issues. For a man who doesn't want his wife to be angry or mistrustful, Dickens stimulates these emotions in a rather provocative manner. At the least it is indiscreet of him to write, in 1838, that he had a "most delicious lady's maid" as a traveling companion for twenty miles, or, on a subsequent trip in 1839, that he had been most attentive to an upholsterer's daughter, or that he had met a young woman in 1846 who didn't suit him, she was not "pretty enough."[22] Knowing Kate's predisposition to be jealous, this kind of gratuitous information reveals a remarkable insensitivity.[23]

A further insensitivity, which places Catherine in a humiliating position, is revealed in a letter from Turin in 1853. In it Dickens alludes to Kate's jealousy of Mme. De la Rue, whom Dickens had treated with mesmerism (for a nervous tic) some nine years earlier. The Turin letter suggests that Catherine write to the la Rues expressing her gratitude for their current hospitality to Dickens.[24] Whether Catherine was correct or not about Dickens' possible intimacy with Mme. De la Rue, Dickens' request is inappropriate. It places Catherine in the position of reviving an interval of mortification. Writing to Mme. De la Rue would have reactivated the memory of her jealousy with its concommitant loss of confidence in Dickens. It would also cause a painful erosion of dignity in carrying out a pretense of cordiality she could not possibly feel. And if Catherine felt herself to have been unduly suspicious about Dickens' earlier association with Mme. De la Rue it would conjure additional shame at having (at that time) created a humiliating situation for Dickens, for the la Rues, and for herself. Dickens' advice about the letter might have been intended as a kind gesture toward the la Rues but it was a thoughtless one to Catherine. And if his relationship with Mme. De la Rue had not been innocent, the suggestion to Catherine was a cruel one.

Dickens is inconsiderate of Kate's feelings in other respects. In a letter from Yarmouth a few years earlier (1849), he writes:

I bought you a shawl at Norwich—I don't think much of it. It's Norwich manufacture.

. . . .

Tell Georgy with my love that I should have bought her one, but I thought she would prefer a muff. She shall have which she likes, in town.

This letter reveals a greater consideration for Georgy's feelings than it does for Kate's. Dickens is not certain that Georgy prefers a muff; he indicates that there is a possibility that she might favor a shawl and therefore, being desirous of pleasing her, he gives her an option, a courtesy he denies to Kate. His comment about the shawl being made in Norwich implies that it is either of an inferior quality, or of a style that is not aesthetically pleasing. If he didn't like it, why did he buy it? The impression the letter gives is that it was just an obligatory present, one to which he gave little thought. Yet, having made the purchase it is unseemly in him to announce his distaste for it. To do so reveals a callous indifference to Kate's sensibilities. Furthermore, to have bought a shawl of inferior quality, design or workmanship is an especial affront to Kate considering the fact that she was an excellent needlewoman, "point-lace being among her accomplishments."[25]

Dickens' letters to Kate are significantly analogous to *Little Dorrit*. Subtle feelings of negativism are discernible in the letters and in the novel; a tone of hostility pervades both. Ambiguities exist in each of the written forms. The letters mark Dickens' insensitivity to Kate; the novel shows Arthur's insensitivity to Amy. The correspondence indicates Kate's distrust of Charles; the novel echoes that feeling in Arthur's suspicion of his mother. The letters record Dickens' humiliation of his wife; the novel portrays Dorrit's abasement of his daughter. The letters show that Dickens stimulates Catherine's jealousy; the novel shows that Amy provokes Fanny's wrath. The negative attitudes and feelings unearthed in Dickens' personal life are revelatory of similar attitudes and feelings in *Little Dorrit*. Linking the man to the artist in her biography of Dickens, Storey quotes Dickens' disillusioned daughter: "We like to think of our geniuses as great characters—but we can't."

A decade after Storey's biography appeared, R. J. Cruikshank, in *Charles Dickens and Early Victorian England* (1949), writes: "For Charles Dickens the year of Pickwick was the beginning of the age of Dickens." Cruikshank admires Dickens' social criticism and praises his "radiant genius" in presenting the lower middle class world. During the nineteen-fifties, commentary began to expand in the direction of Dickens the artist, in addition to Dickens the social critic. But the critical view of the early fifties is generally unflattering. Many commentators express the opinion that Dickens is a "negligible craftsman." A dissenting and penetrating critic, Edgar Johnson, writes in 1952 that the "great structure that [Dickens] finally evolved integrated his [social] criticism into a whole of remarkable intellectual and artistic power."

From the mid-twentieth century to the present, continued interest in Dickens' social criticism has been augmented by an increasing and continued attention to his symbolism, psychology and artistry. In the nineteen-sixties Earle Davis argues that Dickens is a careful craftsman, that his narrative style incorporates symbolic overtones and that he is "indeed, a conscious artist." George Ford notes that the sixties and the seventies saw a spate of critical commentary on the subject of Dickens' art and that keen interest has been evinced in his style and language, in addition to constant attention to characterization. Edgar Johnson agrees with Wilson that in the "entire range of his work Dickens never drew a character with more delicate subtlety and psychological penetration" than William Dorrit. Johnson's successors express a similarly perceptive view about the Father of the Marshalsea, but few critics are as contemplative in evaluating the heroine of *Little Dorrit*. With the exception of a few specialists such as Carlisle, eighties' criticism retains a traditional nineteenth century response to the heroine of *Little Dorrit*. Carlisle, who has long challenged Amy's status as the

Angel in the House, continues to question the heroine's piety.[26] However, from the mid-nineteenth century to the present, the overwhelming critical opinion regarding Amy neglects Dickens' "delicate subtlety and psychological penetration." A staggering number of otherwise brilliant analysts appear to be inadequate in their evaluation of Amy. They have but to look at Dickens' developing awareness of his art to realize that in a novel of his maturity a duplicitous presentation of his heroine is central to the unity of the oeuvre. In a recent article devoted to illusions, Rosenberg remarks that we are cautioned by Dickens in the later works "about trusting appearances at all regardless of the motivations and moral nature of the character being described."[27]

Feminists, mainly, have either overlooked or intentionally disregarded the delineation of Amy as a proper subject of their important concern. She is a perfect illustration of the warping effect of submissiveness, and of the power of literary creation and criticism to establish and to perpetuate stereotypes. In her, Dickens has created, in part, a typical Victorian heroine, which he then carefully and judiciously undermines in order to show the ways in which a character might realistically cope with so oppressive a condition of life as Amy must. Dickens' interweaving of delusory images within the whole portrait of Amy creates reader difficulty in abstracting truth from myth, which in turn causes both the reading and the critiquing of the character to become blurred, an ambiguity that serves Dickens' purpose well, since he is experimenting in the later novel with the concept of anti-heroine and anti-hero, which Amy and Arthur assuredly are. Few critics have noted that Dickens is moving, in some of his later works, toward anti-heroic actions in his heroes.[28]

It is much simpler and more traditional for analysts to say that Dickens has created a biased portrait of Amy than it is to acknowledge that many nineteenth and twentieth century critics are perpetuating a myth about Little Dorrit that Dickens didn't write, or only partially wrote. For over a century such eminent commentators as Whipple, Crotch, Trilling, the Leav-

ises, MacKensies and others have misperceived Amy to be of
unalloyed purity. Suzanne Graver properly reminds us of a
familiar Dickensian technique when she states that subterfuge
is a strategy used by the powerless.[29]

Amy's evasive tactics are also overlooked by Dyson, whose
religious approach to the novel urges readers to believe that
Little Dorrit "is truly Christlike."[30] Yet in the section of his text
immediately preceding this argument Dyson comments on the
goodness of Amy and Arthur in a curious way. He says of the
hero and heroine that though "virtuous, they are—or seem to
be—derelict." To be Christlike and derelict are contradictory.
Amy may be one or the other; she cannot be both. Dyson is
superimposing a religious view on Amy that Dickens was
careful to undercut. He is attending to only some of the
characteristics Dickens invested her with. However, although
he is not consciously observant of some of the subliminal
characteristics which comprise part of Amy's personality, he is
subconsciously reacting to them. If he was not responding to
the inclusion of negative traits in Amy's personality Dyson
would not term her derelict. What Dyson really means is that
Amy is derelict in relation to saintliness and in this he is correct.
She is not angelic; she is human. It is the inclusion of non-
saintly but human foibles in her character which preclude her
being Christlike. What Dyson is responding to without giving
sufficient credence to are Amy's negative characteristics. He is
feeling but overlooking her competitiveness with Fanny, which
induces the heroine to goad her sister into rages; he is unob-
servant of the image of virtue Amy seeks to project whose
function it is to enhance her miniscule power within the family;
he is unaware of the passive hostility in Amy which surfaces in
her teasing of that poor unfortunate character Maggy, and of
Clennam when he is incarcerated.

Interestingly, Amy chooses, in both instances, to mildly
torment those who are exceedingly vulnerable and more unfortunate than she. Two instances are few, but they comprise
an important aspect of Dickens' deceptive characterization of
Amy. These ambiguous instances, generally diagnosed as

innocent ruses, are incorporated into the novel to heighten the effect of Amy's humanity—to make her real. Their function is to undercut the image of Amy as angelic. She is not a religious symbol; she is a representation of human suffering which includes the perversions of personality attendant upon victimization. Dickens has carefully introduced aspects of the Victorian ideal in Amy: her dutifulness, her servitude, her industriousness, and her timidity; but he has also incorporated realistic elements of personality such as deceit, manipulation and passive aggression, which enable her to survive the untenable conditions of her existence. It is these very flaws in her character, including her repressed sexual attraction to Dorrit, which make her human.

On Dickens' estimate of the rewards of virtue, Dyson is perceptive. Commenting on *Little Dorrit* he states that:

> Nowhere else does Dickens produce for virtue a role so inherently exhausting and unrewarding. . . . Nowhere else is his psychological insight into virtue so harrowing: it is a probing of the 'good' of good at its most sensitive point.

In *Little Dorrit* Dickens is ambiguous on the 'good' of good. He presents the Victorian ideals of moral seriousness, duty, self-abnegation and discipline, but he does not affirm that these values result in reward. Although Amy and Arthur move, at the end of the novel, into a "modest life of usefulness and happiness" the rewards of their relative virtue remain dubious. Amy's married life is a return to the drudgery she was conditioned to in her years in the Marshalsea. In summation Dickens is careful to indicate that Amy assumes responsibility not only for her own children but for Fanny's as well. The pattern of Amy's married life is unvaried from the mode of her prison tenure. This is no mythic happy ending; Dickens is saying that life is imprisonment. It is an ending which suggests no exit from anguish, and is evocative of Dickens' bitter disillusionment with life.

Little Dorrit is not, as many critics suggest, a hopeful novel. Nor can Amy freely and easily be Arthur's salvation, as Miller suggests. Although on one level Amy does give purpose to Arthur's life she cannot compensate him for his years of emotional deprivation or give complete meaning to his life. Becoming Doyce's partner could have given meaning to Arthur's life but he destroyed that opportunity by the perverseness with which he neglected to honor Doyce's wishes. Arthur is ultimately reinstated in his job but not because of Arthur's exemplary behavior. It is due solely to Doyce's generous spirit. Perversity is a keynote of Arthur's character which marriage to Amy will not eradicate.

Arthur's passionate obstinacy is overlooked by Trilling's statement that Arthur "has by no means been robbed of his ethical will."[31] Early on in the novel the hero announces this flaw in his character. He proclaims to Mr. Meagles that he lacks volition. Coloring with discomfort, Arthur states, "I have no will" (I, 2, 59). What Arthur really means (which causes his disquiet) is that he lacks volition for positive ethical action. Although he secures employment, he destroys his job by unethical action. His discomfiture resides in the subconscious awareness that his resolve functions primarily in pursuit of negative action. Arthur has been tempted by the thought of speculation and has succumbed to gambling fever. His manipulation of the firm's funds is an act of immoral behavior and of a temporizing will, regardless of the rationalization Arthur offers for his motivation. An element of avarice exists in his gambling and in this respect Arthur is no different from the other characters who wager and are ruined. Arthur has been lured, in part, by the danger inherent in stock transactions—disaster, reprisal, punishment—which is spurred by a perverse desire to exercise his will against his partner's wishes. His stubborn determination contains within it the seed of expected punishment, and the anticipated penalty is forthcoming in his imprisonment.

Trilling is incisive on Arthur's relationship with Mrs. Clennam and its significance to the novel. Commenting on Arthur's obsessive notion of his family's guilt, Trilling relates Arthur's personal malady to the larger social malady. The Circumlocution Office, as an institution representative of the social sickness in England, is not solely to blame for a diseased society. The individual's personal disorders are equally at fault. Noting the complexity of the representation of society in *Little Dorrit*, Trilling states that "the emphasis on the internal life and on personal responsibility is very stong in *Little Dorrit*."[32]

Personal accountability surfaces in a cunningly ambiguous chapter entitled "Little Dorrit's Party," which discloses an underside of Amy's character. It is the chapter in which Amy dresses in a child's clothes when she and Maggy roam the London streets between midnight and dawn. Amy wisely outfits herself to create the impression that Maggy is the mother and she the child. She knows that no man will accost the grotesque Maggy with sexual intent, but also knows that she herself may be a sexual lure. William Burgan points out that her motive for enacting this charade is to prevent rape. It is, Burgan argues, "anything but an expression of childlikeness."[33] Burgan's point, with which I am in accord, is that Little Dorrit is not so sexually innocent nor so ignorant of the sexual facts of life as most critics claim. The cunning quality of her self-protective act indicates a sophisticated degree of awareness of the sexual dangers inherent on the city streets at night. But it also raises a question regarding Amy's free choice. Why does she elect to visit Clennam at midnight, knowing in advance that she'll be locked out of the Marshalsea and therefore will be unprotected on the streets of London? Why does Dickens create this midnight scene for her? He does so to show her awareness of sexuality, and furthermore to reveal an element in her personality which seeks out the danger of a possible sexual encounter. Like Arthur, she is lured into gambling, but the risk to her is sexual rather than monetary. Once again Dickens is depicting the attraction of danger which partially motivates a character's actions. He is showing Amy's ambivalence about danger. She is drawn toward a potential hazard and simultaneously seeks to protect herself from that peril. If Dickens wanted to present an ideal of Victorian womanhood (or child-womanhood) he would have created a daylight scene. To insure the presentation of Amy as representative of the Victorian ideal he would have logically had her visit Clennam, not at midnight, but in the daytime, since she did not have a daily job and was therefore partially free during the day.

In *Dickens The Novelist*, the Leavises convey their regard for the psychology and artistry of *Little Dorrit*, terming it a masterpiece which "it would be fatuous to suppose he achieved accidentally and unconsciously and without knowing it." The Leavises' position on Dickens' insight and art is well-grounded. They are equally effective in their assessment of Dickens' concern with reality and on his capacity for "profound and subtle thought." Perceptively commenting on the secondary characters in *Little Dorrit*, the Leavises note that each of the characters "plays a contributory part, in inviting us to make notes on his or her distinctive 'value' in relation to the whole." One of the most important secondary characters is Miss Wade, whose value derives from the contrast in pathology she presents relative to the other more subtly disordered personalities in the novel. Late and mid-twentieth century critics view Miss Wade with more sophisticated responses than did early twentieth century commentators. Representing the earlier view is Gissing who remarks at the turn of the century, that *Little Dorrit* "shows us, or aims at showing us Miss Wade and Tattycoram, from both of whom we turn incredulous." Although Gissing acknowledges that *Little Dorrit* contains some of Dickens' best writing, he does not comprehend Dickens' penetrating psychological realism. In Miss Wade, Dickens reveals the distortion of personality that can issue from the pain of abandonment; in Tattycoram, the novelist depicts the despair attendant upon the character's dichotomous identity.

In the mid-twentieth century Johnson, Trilling and Miller's criticisms are representative of a more sympathetic analysis of Miss Wade's condition and function to the novel as a whole. Johnson notes Miss Wade's relation to the overriding theme of imprisonment which permeates *Little Dorrit*. Miss Wade personifies the ultimate state of immurement. "Her jail is purely a state of mind, but from it she can never emerge." Trilling

observes that it is part of the complexity of *Little Dorrit* which
"deals so bitterly with society that those of its characters who
share its social bitterness are by that very fact condemned." Yet
conversely Miss Wade and Tattycoram elicit our sympathy for,
as Trilling incisively argues, Tatty's wrath is not wholly unjus-
tified by her ambiguous position in the Meagles' household,
and Miss Wade's paranoia has been induced by a loveless
childhood. Miller divulges the core of Miss Wade's personality
by specifying her personality disorder in current psychological
terminology. He assesses her as sado-masochistic, and observes that the many forms of incarceration in this novel are
primarily spiritual rather than physical. The correct consensus
of recent criticism of the secondary characters is that they are
particularizations of the overriding theme of imprisonment.
Each character is immured in his own personal disorder.

Dickens' cunning technique in presenting the blatant pathology of Miss Wade as part of his deceptive methodology has not
been given the attention it warrants. Quiller-Couch, while
remarking on what he considers the unnecessary intrusion of
Miss Wade into *Little Dorrit* states: "Often as I have read [*Little
Dorrit*] I should be gravelled if asked, at this moment, to tell
you . . . what Miss Wade and Tattycoram have to do with the
story." Approximately a quarter of a century later, Monod,
using almost the identical terminology, arrives at the same
conclusion.[34] The fact that Dickens did not intend Miss Wade to
be an unnecessary intrusion but created her as an intrinsic part
of the novel may be seen in a letter to Forster in which Dickens
states:

> In Miss Wade I had an idea, which I thought a new one, of making the
> introduced story so fit into surroundings impossible of separation from
> the main story, as to make the blood of the book circulate through both.

Citing Dickens' letter to Forster, Monod argues that Dickens
failed in his attempt.

However, Miss Wade's function in the novel serves as
contrast—between her obvious negative characteristics and the
more subtle negative characteristics of Amy and Arthur. The

contrastive juxtaposition allows the reader to focus on the expressed personality disorder of Miss Wade and to disregard the veiled personality disorders of hero and heroine. This again is part of Dickens' deceptive methodology, to slight the connection between central and subsidiary characters. While the inclusion of Miss Wade enhances the whole tone of bitterness of the book, it misdirects the reader away from the unwholesome traits of the protagonists. Miss Wade is protrayed as obviously mentally disturbed, with the implication that she feels hatred and rebuffs kindnesses which Amy and Arthur don't do. It is her flagrant misinterpretations of other characters which dull the reader's awareness of the link between her actions and those of Amy and Arthur. As Miss Wade repels all attempts at kindness, Arthur rejects Mrs. Clennam's overtures of hospitality and Amy rebuffs Fanny's demonstrations of affection. By comparison with Miss Wade, Amy and Arthur are relatively appropriate in their behavior, but they exhibit, to a minor degree, the perversity which Dickens highlights in his psychologically realistic portrait of Miss Wade.

The character whom Miss Wade attempts and succeeds temporarily in luring away from her expected role is Tattycoram. Tatty represents another form of imprisonment due, as Randolph Splitter observes, to the conflict attendant upon her ambiguous role in the Meagleses' family.[35] Functioning as servant-sister to Pet and servant-daughter to the Meagleses, Tatty cannot endure the divided self which her condition imposes. Trilling sees Tatty as the victim of indifferent foster parents. However, a close reading of the text indicates that the Meagleses are not indifferent; they are misguided. Mr. Meagles devotes considerable attention to Tatty's passionate outbursts, but he doesn't understand the poignancy of her dichotomous position, and his lack of perception makes him seem indifferent to her pain.

Tatty's rage at those whom she considers to be her oppressors is turned inward, and she inflicts punishment on herself. Splitter convincingly argues that Tatty's masochism demonstrates her inner conflict. It is a self-punitory act for experienc-

ing hatred against those who are simultaneously her oppressors and her benefactors. She is also retaliating against herself
for her wrathful outbursts which she knows to be socially
inappropriate.

Dickens presents Tatty as a character who is defying appropriate standards of Victorian behavior. Trilling sees Tatty's
bitterness as a perversion of the desire for love.[37] It is more
likely the result of her thwarted desire for equality and acceptance. Dickens is crying out against imprisonment, spiritual as
well as physical. Tattycoram reinforces the image that life is
immurement and that even when one attempts to escape, as
Tatty does, there is no exit. Tatty has to and does make a
compromise in returning to the Meagleses. She knows that Mr.
Meagles will not change, for he cannot understand her despair
at being, to some extent, a non-person in his household. To the
best of his meager ability (which his name suggests) Mr.
Meagles attempts to be a good parent.

Writing on the representation of the good parent in *Little
Dorrit*, Hobsbaum cites Mr. Meagles as one of its few examples.
The other is old Mr. Nandy who incarcerates himself voluntar-
ily in the Poor House rather than to impose himself on his
children. Hobsbaum's theory of Nandy is enlightening, but his
analysis of Meagles misses the subtlety of Dickens' presentation. In *"Little Dorrit," A Reader's Guide to Charles Dickens* (1972)
Hobsbaum states that Mr. Meagles is a good parent because he
allows Pet to exercise her will regardless of the consequences.
However, Dickens is taking a position against the permissive
behavior of Mr. Meagles, which despite his love, is harmful to
his daughter. Dickens is indicating that Meagles' permissive
rearing of his daughter results in disastrous consequences to
her. Meagles lavishes too much in goods and services on Pet,
and his life is too much occupied in anticipating her every
desire. By not restraining her in some manner, he abrogates his
responsibility as a parent. Dickens is saying that in order to
qualify as a good parent, Meagles must place reasonable
restraints on Pet's will.

Although Meagles truly loves his daughter, it is a misguided affection, which ultimately plays a role in her calamitous marriage. Any disquiet that Pa Meagles may feel at his daughter's nuptials is not untinctured by his pride in Gowan's social status. Meagles' snobbishness precludes any discussion of his ambivalent feelings regarding the marriage. Stanley Tick makes the dubious observation that Meagles "is to be commended for his . . . wisdom insofar as he permits his daughter to choose for herself the man she most desires." It is more reasonable to argue that it is not wisdom but ambition that directs Meagles' silence on the subject. He wants to align himself (however remotely) with the aristocracy. Peter Christmas quite properly reminds us that "Father and daughter together tie [the] knot"[38] of her unfortunate union. Pet is ultimately immured in a dismal relationship by her own misguided choice and by her father's complicity. Meagles' snobbishness has conspired to imprison him, as well as his daughter, in an unhappy familial relationship with the child he loves, with her in-laws and with her supercilious husband.

Tick further argues that Meagles is representative of goodness because he is portrayed in a pastoral setting at Twickenham which depicts "Arcadian Virtues," and that despite its eccentricity Twickenham is a contrast to the grim abodes of other characters in *Little Dorrit*. Tick neglects to mention the Plornishes' Happy Cottage, another eccentricity, which truly houses a virtuous family. The Plornishes exhibit moral excellence before they acquire their Happy Cottage. They are virtuous in poverty. And Mr. Plornish is not seen weighing and balancing his fortune, as is Mr. Meagles, whose scale is a fixture on his desk. Meagles' scale is a symbol of greed, which no longer manifests itself in the acquisition of money. It is unnecessary since he has a sufficiency. His avarice takes another form. He becomes acquisitive in relation to status.

Although the Plornishes' Happy Cottage is a fiction, it is as real to Mrs. Plornish as Twickenham is to Mr. Meagles. And Meagles, who considers himself a practical man, also engages in a little fiction relevant to his home. He demands that the house always be in readiness to receive him, as though he were about to return to it that very day, while he sojourns indefinitely on the Continent. Mr. Meagles has the financial resources to employ a housekeeper to help him maintain his harmless illusion. The Plornishes have no monetary resources. In "Time and the Circle in *Little Dorrit*," Roopnaraine is precise in remarking that "the Plornishes are at once the most economically deprived and the most harmonious of the families portrayed."

Among the families delineated in *Little Dorrit* minimal critical recognition has been given to the function of Mr. F.'s Aunt in the Casby household. Until recently commentary has mainly ignored this important secondary character, except as parody. Recent critics such as Wilde (1964), Stang (1970), and Splitter (1977) have begun to rectify the lapse. Wing (1977) however, finds her simply to be a joke, observing that to attach any other significance to her is "to kill [the] joke stone dead."[39] Wing's interpretation neglects the symbolic ingenuity with which Dickens has rendered Mr. F.'s Aunt. Although he portrays her as an eccentric she functions as a vehicle for Flora's hostility. Because the Aunt is old she can, with impunity, say things that decorum does not permit Flora to utter. And since the Aunt is cryptic, her hostile remarks tend to be dismissed as rancorous non-sequiturs. Her position in the novel is accorded greater status by Wilde, who comes closer than Wing to understanding her role. Wilde calls her the "irrational symbol of all the world's aggression."[40] Nonetheless, Wilde's reading is not quite precise. It is more accurate to note that she is the symbolic representation of Flora's hostility to Arthur. In this role she functions as Flora's alter ego, providing an outlet for some of the unexpressed rage that Flora feels about Arthur's rejection of her. In reciprocity, the Aunt receives the protection and loving care that Flora administers to her.

Furthermore, it is inaccurate to say, as Splitter does, that Dickens' comedic characters tend to resemble stock comic types. He writes that in its "most extreme form (Mr. F.'s Aunt) the Dickensian humor is a robot-like machine entirely cut off from human conscious control."[41] Mr. F.'s Aunt is perfectly aware of what she is saying and she is constant and consistent in expressing it. When she declares that she hates a fool (I, 13, 200) she is directing her animosity at Arthur and telling him that he lacks sense. When, at a subsequent meeting she initiates another rancorous remark aimed at Arthur, she is pursuing the same theme. Declaring that "There's mile-stones on the Dover Road!" (I, 23, 314) she is reminding Arthur that he recently had to cross the English Channel from France, probably taking the Dover Road to London. Since Dover is a principal port of passenger communication across the Channel it's a reasonable assumption that Arthur disembarked there on his return to England from France, traversing the Dover Road to London. Returning to London was a significant event for him, after having been away so long. Another milestone, should he elect to accept it, would be to marry Flora. But the Aunt intuitively knows that he will not do so, which is why she discharges her verbal missile at him with the "utmost abhorrence" (I, 23, 319). Still harping on the same subject of Arthur's stupidity, she scorns him for his repudiation of her niece and is steadfast in her rage at him for his refusal to court Flora a second time. Considering the Aunt's reciprocal relationship with her niece and her recognition of Arthur's romantic disinterest in Flora, the Aunt makes a quite conscious human effort to show both her disdain to Arthur and her loyalty to Flora.

Although in *"Little Dorrit*: A World in Reverse," Stang regards the Aunt's cryptic remarks as pertinent, surprisingly he calls her "one of the most extreme cases of dehumanization in literature." Whereas the Aunt's outward appearance (her staring wooden-doll face) gives the impression of non-human qualities, her volatile and expressive emotions are not indicative of a divestiture of her individuality or her human attributes. Stang is misreading Mr. F.'s Aunt. He is evaluating her primarily on the basis of her surface traits, disregarding one of the psychologically valid sources of her volatility. For the Aunt, Arthur acts as an outlet for her rage, which is ready to be triggered by his presence or by an allusion to him. His name need only be inferred (such as occcurs in the pie shop) and she voices her enduring contempt of him by saying "Bring him for'ard and I'll chuck him out o' winder!" (II, 34, 889). In her ostensible non-sequiturs she is merely picking up the thread of previous conversations with or about Arthur. She is expanding upon and reinforcing her disdain of him, a theme which preoccupies her mind.

Whereas the Aunt's speech manifests (amid her general hostility) a special obsession with Arthur, it is a reflection in part of her own personal disorder; it is not a dehumanization of her. As Wing and other critics have observed, mental disturbance forms a rudimentary motif for *Little Dorrit*. Mr. F.'s Aunt is an integral part of the unity of theme which depicts psychological dysfunctions in *Little Dorrit*. Mr. F.'s Aunt is not one of Dickens' caricatured immortals who stand out in the memory solely as humorous eccentrics. She carries forward the general design of a book whose structure is based on the principle of hostility. She is as imprisoned by her rage as Mrs. Clennam is by her paralysis, or as Dorrit is by the bars of the Marshalsea and by the imprint of his quarter-century of immurement.

Symbolic imprisonment extends beyond the trauma inflicted on the Dorrits by the Marshalsea. It is inherent in the linguistics of communication. John Romano advances the cogent thesis that language itself presents a form of confinement. Language is held in restraint "not by the prison-like world it represents in *Little Dorrit* . . . but by the prison-like exigencies of language itself."[42]

One manifestation of Dickens' attempt to escape from the confines of language appears in his creation of Flora Finching's monologues, to which numerous twentieth-century poets owe an unacknowledged debt. Flora's kaleidoscopic diction is an effort to break through the formal conventions of speech, to liberate her from the imprisoning dictates of grammatical structure. When Flora visits Dorrit, the legatee, to make inquiries about Rigaud's disappearance, she feels uncertain about her social status relative to Dorrit's. In order to elevate her self-image, she engages in a power play with Dorrit, in which she inadvertently reveals her state of mind and emotions. In a style

which admits of little regard for syntax, Flora alludes to William
in her remarks that:

> one possessed of such knowledge of life as no doubt with so many
> changes must have been acquired, for Mr. F. himself said frequently
> that although well educated in the neighborhood of Blackheath at as
> high as eighty guineas which is a good deal for parents and the plate
> kept back too on going away but that is more a meanness than its value.
>
> (II, 17, 680)

Flora attempts to articulate three ideas in this vertiginous
speech. First, she compliments Dorrit on his wisdom about life.
The purpose of the flattery is to make him amenable to her suit.
Second, she reminds him by the phrase "so many changes"
that he has been a debtor. The aim of mentioning his ignominious past is to revive in him the memory that he too was once
a petitioner in need of assistance and that he then felt as
helpless as she does in begging a favor. Third, she quickly
changes the subject, retreating from the unkind allusion to his
past, because on a subconscious level she knows it to be
ungenerous. By referring to her dead husband's lineage she
hopes to enhance her prestige via their wealth. She indicates
that her in-laws were people of financial substance by explicitly
stating the cost of her husband's education; but by emphasiz-
ing that they didn't present their son with the plate when he
left home, she is ascribing a meanness to her in-laws, which is
not her intent. She wants to present her in-laws, and by
extension herself, in a favorable light. To cast doubt on their
generosity is to undercut her intention. So that what Dickens is
actually saying is that even while Flora attempts to liberate
herself linguistically by ignoring grammatical structure, she
imprisons herself in another way. Since her style lacks restraint, she reveals more than she should, which prevents her
from achieving the self-image she wants to create. Paradoxically, her language both frees and fetters her.

The language of fiction is the focus of Janice Carlisle's fine
essay, "*Little Dorrit*: Necessary Fictions," in which Carlisle
properly reminds us that the term "fiction" shares a common
root with "feign," which signifies something artificial rather

than real. In its most pejorative sense fiction is a lie. In *Little Dorrit* equivocation is seen as one of the less virtuous character traits of the protagonist. Describing Amy as an unconventional heroine with regard to her equivocal nature, Carlisle states that Amy's "lies are like the lies the novelist tells. . . . Like Little Dorrit, Dickens fails to confront certain facts, he ignores certain problems." This is substantially true. Dickens exercises selectivity in determining the information to impart or to withhold in order to unify the structure of his work. In fact, Carlisle's recent critical theory of Dickens' deceptiveness restates a critical point of view that was expounded in 1858 by John Cordy Jeaffreson. Jeaffreson writes that Dickens "makes use of . . . those facts of life which will tend to arouse the required emotions . . . but still it is not the whole—and the result is a deception."

Philip Collins also remarks on "Dickens' unwillingness or inability to express the whole truth (as he knew it) in his fiction."[43] Collins' complaint confounds truth with art. His statement disregards the process of creative discrimination necessary to the structure of Dickens' fictional works. Dickens himself reveals his thoughts on creative selectivity when he responds to a potential contributor to *Household Words*. Offering detailed advice to Miss Emily Jolly, Dickens argues that:

> The people do not talk as such people would; and the . . . subtle touches of description which [would make] the scene real . . . are wanting. The more you set yourself to the illustration of your heroine's passionate nature, the more indispensable this . . . atmosphere of truth becomes. . . . I have no means of knowing whether you are patient in the pursuit of this art. . . . When one is impelled to write this or that, one has still to consider: How much of this will tell for what I mean? How much . . . remains that is truly belonging to this ideal character and these ideal circumstances?[44]

Dickens' comments to Miss Jolly reveal a primary consideration not with truth, but with art. He stresses the need for unity in a fictitious work, in which the component parts of the fiction cohere to form a unified structure. He advocates the use of more realistic dialogue for the kinds of characters she is portraying; description which accords with and enhances the reality of her scenes; and psychological validity in the characterization of her heroine. His phrase "atmosphere of truth" is an important part of his credo for art. An atmosphere of truth is not truth; it is a fiction, a representation of truth. Dickens is espousing a literary device of verisimilitude; he is not suggesting the truth of a confessional (as Collins' complaint would seem to want him to do). In mentioning patience, Dickens is referring to the discipline which is essential to the creation of a work of art. His interrogation "How much of this will tell for what I mean?" asks Miss Jolly to consider the amount of information she incorporates or deletes from her manuscript in order to reveal her meaning. Suggesting that she contemplate what is truly belonging to an ideal character and circumstance, Dickens is not using the term "ideal" in its abstract connotation of a perfect model. He employs the term as a standard of excellence within the confines of Miss Jolly's vision of the character and of the world she is defining.

Harry Stone presents a comprehensive and penetrating analysis on the subject of Dickens and art. Stone writes that "Dickens viewed art as a deeply social force, as a way of humanizing life, but he also felt that art satisfied profound psychological and aesthetic needs."[45] Harvey Sucksmith examines Dickens' novels in terms of rhetorical art. Sucksmith provides evidence that "Dickens' insistence on discipline, on the conscious direction of emotion and energy . . . indicate the traditional view of art as rhetoric . . . a responsible striving . . . for the best effect."[46] In his opening chapter of *Little Dorrit* Dickens' "conscious direction of emotion and energy" achieves an immediate and complex effect. The description of the stultifying air of the August day reinforces the description of the oppressive atmosphere of the prison. Simultaneously, the glare of the Marseilles sun contrasts with the semi-darkness of the damp jail, carrying forward opposing themes of light and dark, heat and cold, freedom and imprisonment during humanity's destined confinement by nature, self, and society.

Dickens pursues the theme of confinement to which the human condition is subject throughout the two volumes of the novel. Dorrit is constrained in poverty and in wealth, behind bars and in his free state. His physical being is held in constraint by the architectural structure of the Marshalsea, and his psychic being is immured in emotional disorders even after his period of physical liberation. His daughter is, on some level, similarly chained. Her future is confined within her past. From the opening lines of the book to its conclusion, Dickens is saying that man is in some measure in fetters. Roopnaraine captures part of the essence of Dickens' bleak vision in *Little Dorrit* in his analysis of the last lines of the novel. Roopnaraine writes convincingly that:

> The ending is achingly devoid of . . . anything that is even potentially redemptive. The final sentence, with its slow, measured cadence, cheats us of those feelings of relief and elation which the happy ending should generate. . . . We are left with the empty feeling that out of the wreckage of so many dreams and the waste of so many lives, this is all we can salvage "a modest life of usefulness and happiness."[47]

Roopnaraine is substantially correct but not quite precise in his analysis. Redemption for Amy and Arthur is relative.[48]

Dickens' resolution of *Little Dorrit* enunciates a compromise with life. The reality of the Clennams' future may be charted in terms of their past. Their histories are unalterable; their personalities formed. Carlisle reminds us that Arthur and Amy begin their married life with a deception. Little Dorrit burns the documents that would make known to Arthur his mother's unethical behavior. Amy's stealthy act is done out of love for Arthur; nevertheless, it carries with it a seed of deceit at the inception of their union. Dickens' purpose in creating this ambiguous act for his protagonist is to emphasize the fact that Amy will continue to function in marriage, as she did in her unwed state, in a secretive manner. Dickens is saying that despite the healing properties of love, Arthur and Amy can effectuate only a relative alteration of the life they had previously known. They cannot magically recreate themselves or their histories. They are bound to a significant degree by their pasts. In his imagistic rendering of the "sunshine and shade" into which the couple moves at the close of the novel, Dickens is continuing the contrast of the freedom and imprisonment theme with which the book opens. This thematic continuity reveals Dickens' grim recognition of the constraints placed upon humankind and of the forceful energy of a past that might realistically trespass upon the present and future of his protagonists.

Notes

[1] G. K. Chesterton, *Appreciations and Criticisms of the Works of Charles Dickens* (1911; rpt. New York: Kennikat, 1966), p. 183. Although Chesterton acknowledges that *LD* contains some of Dickens' best writing he deprecates this novel in terms of its absence of form and theme, pp. 178–80.

[2] Stephen Leacock, *Charles Dickens: His Life and Work* (New York: Doubleday-Doran, 1934), p. 191. Leacock follows Chesterton in his general admiration for Dickens but his response to *LD* is also negative, p. 146.

[3] Wilson's essay focuses on the social and psychological influences affecting Dickens' views on children. Angus Wilson, "Dickens on Childhood and Children," *Dickens 1970: Centenary Essays*, ed. Michael Slater (London: Chapman and Hall, 1970), pp. 218–19.

[4] Among *LD*'s detractors see Albert S. G. Canning, *Philosophy of Charles Dickens* (London: Smith, 1880), pp. 288–308. Although the prevailing nineteenth-century approach to *LD* is aesthetic, Canning combines the aesthetic with the philosophical and the social in his analysis of this novel. Canning's thesis is that *LD* is inferior to Dickens' other works in every literary respect, including its lack of power. But he praises Dickens' aim in writing for its effort to draw people of all classes together for the common good. For a more universal extension of Dickens' literary aim see Surveyer, who indicates that Dickens tries to establish bonds of comradeship not only among the various English classes but also between the English people and the French people via the French translations of his works. Edouard Fabre Surveyer, *Dickens in France* (London: The Dickensian, 1932), p. 24.

[5] Von W. H. Riehl [George Eliot], "Art II.—The Natural History of German Life," *The Westminster Review* (London: John Chapman, 1856), 10, 55. Collins attributes this review to George Eliot. Philip Collins, *Dickens: The Critical Heritage* (New York: Barnes and Noble, 1971), p. 343.

[6] Robert L. Patten, *Charles Dickens and His Publishers* (Oxford: Clarendon, 1978), p. 391. A statistical discrepancy appears within Patten's text; on p. 391 he states that 63,000 copies of *LD* were sold, but on p. 432 he claims that only 38,000 copies were printed. It is difficult to envision the sale of almost double the number of copies printed.

[7] John Cordy Jeaffreson, *Novels and Novelists: From Elizabeth to Victoria* (London: Hurst and Blackett, 1858), p. 306. Jeaffreson's panegyric to Dickens'

artistry includes a fine discussion of Dickens' style, characterization and psychology.

8 Andrew Lang, "Introduction," *Little Dorrit* by Charles Dickens (London: Chapman and Hall, 1897), p. viii. Lang's approach to *LD* is three-fold. He combines the aesthetic with the biographical and the psychological approach, accounting for the book's weakness by attributing it to Dickens' unhappy marriage. For an apologetic interpretation of *LD* in terms of Dickens' mental state at the time of writing *LD*, see Chesterton's *Appreciations and Criticisms*, p. 181. For an antithetical view to Lang and Chesterton, see Gissing's discussion of *LD* as one of Dicken's best novels. George Gissing, *Charles Dickens: A Critical Study* (New York: Dodd, Mead, 1904), pp. 98–100.

9 In fact, Miller's premise explores the theme of unity further, in terms of unity within the canon based on Dickens' vision of the world. J. Hillis Miller, *Charles Dickens: The World of His Novels* (1958; rpt. Bloomington: Indiana Univ. Press, 1969), p. 227.

10 Steven Smith, *Public and Private Value: Studies in the Nineteenth Century Novel* (Cambridge: Cambridge UP, 1984), 75.

11 Edmund Wilson, "Dickens: The Two Scrooges," *The Wound and the Bow* (1940; rpt. New York: Oxford UP, 1947), p. 3. For important early twentieth century minority opinions in terms of the excellence of *LD* see: Quiller-Couch who compares Dickens with Shakespeare. Quiller-Couch considers Dickens the greatest of English novelists and *LD* Dickens' most undeservedly devalued book. Arthur Quiller-Couch, *Dickens and Other Victorians* (Cambridge: Cambridge UP, 1927), p. 28.

12 Wilson, *Wound and Bow*, p. 51. A little more than a decade earlier Margharita Widdows analyzed Dickens in terms of his psychological insight using almost the identical phraseology as Wilson. Surprisingly, Wilson doesn't credit Widdows. See Margharita Widdows, *English Literature* (London: Chatto and Windus, 1928), p. 278.

13 For a provocative essay on the reality of prison life in the nineteenth century, see Angus Easson, "Marshalsea Prisoners: Mr. Dorrit and Mr. Hemens," *Dickens Studies Annual*, ed. Robert B. Partlow, Jr. (Carbondale: Southern Illinois Univ. Press, 1974), 3, 77–86. Easson cites the case of an actual prisoner, Mr. Hemens, a man of Dorrit's pretentiousness, and shows the ostracism to which such a personality was subjected by other prisoners. It is Easson's discerning perception that Dickens created Dorrit's position in the Marshalsea as an artistic invention rather than as a factual presentation of prison life.

14 Humphry House, *The Dickens World* (1941; rpt. London: Oxford Univ. Press, 1942), p. 55. House approaches Dickens' works in terms of their importance as historical documents.

15 Randolph Splitter, "Guilt and the Trappings of Melodrama in *Little Dorrit*," *Dickens Studies Annual*, ed. Robert B. Partlow, Jr. (Carbondale: Southern Illinois Univ. Press, 1977), 6, 132–3. Splitter's Freudian approach to

LD argues that the book is a melodramatic attempt on Dickens' part to liberate himself from repression. For a fine distinction between Victorian melodrama and Dickens' "melodramatizing" in *LD*, see Karl Kroeber, *Styles in Fictional Structure*, (Princeton: Princeton UP, 1971), p. 135.

[16] Albert D. Hutter, "Reconstruction Autobiography: The Experience at Warren's Blacking," *Dickens Studies Annual*, ed. Robert B. Partlow, Jr. (Carbondale: Southern Illinois Univ. Press, 1977), 6, 2.

[17] Edgar Johnson, *Charles Dickens: His Tragedy and Triumph* (New York: Simon and Schuster, 1952), p. 679. Johnson graciously terms Dickens' natural rage at John and Elizabeth Dickens, Charles' contradictory sentiments about his parents.

[18] Johnson, *Tragedy and Triumph*, p. 20. Dickens not only lost Fanny to the world of music and education, but he suffered the loss of another important relationship at the same time. When the family left Chatham, Charles had to leave his beloved schoolmaster William Giles, Jr., a man who had seen a special precocity in Charles and who had nurtured it.

[19] Arthur Washburn Brown, *Sexual Analysis of Dickens' Props* (New York: Emerson, 1971), p. 166. Brown's approach to Dickens is strictly Freudian. Brown speciously indicates that Dickens' novels ought to be read in conjunction with Freud's *Interpretation of Dreams* in order to understand the sexual significance of Dickens' characters. Although Brown notes the connection of Dickens' props with sexual imagery in his novels, Brown neglects to mention the iron bars of the Marshalsea as a phallic symbol, one which Amy kisses on the night of her outing, in the chapter titled "Little Dorrit's Party."

[20] For a spiritual approach to the double role of father-son, mother-daughter to which Amy and Arthur aspire, see Richard Barickman, The Spiritual Journey of Amy Dorrit and Arthur Clennam: "A Way Wherein There Is No Ecstasy," *Dickens Studies Annual*, (Carbondale: Southern Illinois Univ. Press, 1978), 7, 181.

[21] *Mr. and Mrs. Charles Dickens: His Letters to Her*, ed. Walter Dexter (New York: Haskell, 1972), p. 22. See especially (a) the letter of March 6, 1836 in which Charles responds to a similar rebuke from Kate, p. 60; (b) letter of Tuesday morning, 1835, p. 12.

[22] Dexter, p. 121. Letter from Charles who was in England, to Catherine who was in Paris. The letters reveal frequent geographical distance between Charles and Kate.

[23] See Dickens' letter to Miss Mary Boyle (1855) in terms of the pattern of provocative behavior he engages in. Dickens' letter to Miss Boyle contains more than cordiality. There is a hint of inappropriate sexual teasing in it and an ambiguous message of a jealousy-provoking nature. Dickens' letter encloses a kiss to Mary, requesting that she return it when done with it. Then after some news about his activities he informs her, "I should have lost my heart to the beautiful young landlady of my hotel (age twenty-nine, dress,

black frock and jacket, exquisitely braided) if it had not been safe in your possession." Dickens' provocative references to other women in his letters might tend to leave the recipient of his letters (whether the recipient be Kate or Miss Boyle) off balance with regard to the sincerity of his affection for the person to whom he is writing. See *The Letters of Charles Dickens*, eds. Georgina Hogarth and Mamie Dickens (New York: Scribner's, 1879), I, 446.

24 Dexter, *Letters*, p. 229. In 1844, Dickens had frequently visited Mme. De la Rue at unconventional hours, which had vexed Kate. She had demanded that Dickens stop seeing and treating Mme. De la Rue and Dickens confided Kate's jealousy to the la Rues. Reference to the Turin letter of 1853 is made by Johnson who views the la Rue situation as humiliating to Dickens. See Johnson, *Tragedy and Triumph*, p. 555. Undoubtedly the situation was embarrassing for Dickens, but Johnson doesn't address the fact that the letter Dickens asks Kate to write to the la Rues places her in an equally uncomfortable position.

25 Gladys Storey, *Dickens and Daughter* (London: Muller, 1939), p. 22. Storey's biographical approach to Catherine Dickens is presented from the perspective of Catherine's daughter, Kate Perugini. The picture disclosed of Catherine reveals a different side of Dickens' wife from that of the inept woman whom we see in the Johnson biography. A more recent biography of Dickens by the MacKenzies is a modification of the Storey and Johnson works. Storey reveals Catherine victimized by Dickens' tyranny, and Johnson pictures Dickens irritated by Catherine's ineptitude. The MacKenzies incorporate both points of view. The three biographies indicate a possible dubeity of evidence but are valuable in terms of their different approaches and perspectives. See Norman and Jeanne MacKenzie, *Dickens: A Life* (Oxford: Oxford Univ. Press, 1979). For the most current biography of Dickens, one that incorporates new epistolary evidence of Dickens' relationship with Kate, see Michael Slater's text, *Dickens and Women* (Stanford: Stanford Univ. Press, 1983). Slater's perceptive evaluation of Dickens' self-delusion in his interactions with his wife adds immeasurably to our understanding of Dickens the man, and the novelist.

26 Janice Carlisle, *The Sense of an Audience: Dickens, Thackery and George Eliot at Mid-Century* (Athens: Univ. of Georgia Press, 1981), 63.

27 Brian Rosenberg, "Vision into Language: The Style of Dickens' Characterization," in *Dickens Quarterly*, II, 4 (Dec. 1985), 122–3.

28 Irwin Weiser, "Reformed But Unrewarded: Pip's Progress," in *Dickens Studies Newsletter* XIV, 4 (Dec. 1983), 143.

29 Suzanne Graver, "Writing in a 'Womanly' Way and the Double Vision of *Bleak House*" in *Dickens Quarterly*, 4 (March 1987), 3.

30 A. E. Dyson, *The Inimitable Dickens* (London: Macmillan, 1970), p. 211. Dyson's thesis is a consideration of the organic structure of each of Dickens'

novels as an autonomous entity, yet one which forms a part of the unity of the canon.

[31] Lionel Trilling, *The Opposing Self* (New York: Harcourt, 1955), p. 53. Trilling's psychological, symbolic and social approach to *LD* sees the self as imprisoned by the culture.

[32] Trilling, p. 49. Trilling's analysis of personal responsibility in *LD* is perceptive, but it does not accord with his disregard of Arthur's moral obligation to his business partner. For another specious analysis which exonerates Arthur in terms of his lack of liability in business, see Earle Davis, "Dickens and Significant Tradition," *Dickens Studies Annual* (Carbondale: Southern Illinois Univ. Press, 1978), 7, 61–2.

[33] William Burgan, "People in the Setting of *Little Dorrit*," *Texas Studies in Language and Literature* (Austin: Univ. of Texas, 1973), p. 115. Burgan's essay concentrates on characters in chance encounters with major characters, such as the prostitute's meeting with Amy, which serves to reveal the ambiguous role of child-woman that Amy plays.

[34] Monod, *Dickens the Novelist*, p. 420. Surprisingly, Monod misinterprets and misunderstands Tattycoram's and Miss Wade's functions in the novel while simultaneously acknowledging the "increasingly complex and delicate feelings and emotions" depicted in *LD*, p. 422.

[35] Splitter, "Guilt and Trappings of Melodrama," p. 125. Splitter quite properly reminds us that Tattycoram functions in part as Miss Wade's double, a reflection of herself as a younger woman. In addition, Tatty sees the older woman as a reflection of her future self.

[36] Splitter, "Guilt and Trappings of Melodrama," p. 127. Tatty, an orphan of unknown parentage, impresses upon the reader the consequences of illegitimacy and the uncertainty a child feels about his mysterious origins.

[37] Trilling, *Opposing Self*, p. 52. For Dickens the unhappy child is the perfect vehicle by which to record his concern with injustice. Additionally, Dickens' abiding interest in abused or neglected children is, in psychological terms, a projection of Dickens' youthful self onto the child character.

[38] Peter Christmas, "*Little Dorrit*: The End of Good and Evil," *Dickens Studies Annual* (Carbondale: Southern Illinois Univ. Press, 1977), 6, 135. Christmas reasonably argues that because Pet has been spoiled, she is therefore vulnerable to Gowan's questionable charms and blind to his obvious flaws. For an opposing view of Pet as the sole person responsible for her predicament, see Hobsbaum, "Little Dorrit," *A Reader's Guide*, p. 208.

[39] George Wing, "Mr. F.'s Aunt: A Laughing Matter," *English Studies in Canada*, 3, (1977), 207–8.

[40] Alan Wilde, "Mr. F.'s Aunt and the Analogical Structure of *Little Dorrit*," *Nineteenth Century Fiction*, 19 (1964), 37. A fuller exploration of the symbolic function of Mr. F.'s Aunt, in terms of hostility, appears in Chapter III.

[41] See Paul B. Davis, "Dickens, Hogarth and the Illustrated *Great Expecta-*

tions," The Dickensian, 80, 3, (Autumn, 1984), 137. Davis notes that Dickens "insisted that his characters were not monstrous caricatures but were human figures drawn from life and modeled on human beings."

[42] John Romano, *Dickens and Reality* (New York: Columbia Univ. Press, 1978), p. 106. Flora's oral pattern of communication establishes its own structure, which the Leavises observe to be "essentially sequential and coherent." See Leavises, *Dickens The Novelist,* p. 241.

[43] Philip Collins, *Dickens and Crime,* (Bloomington: Indiana UP, 1962), p. 114. Collins' text focuses primarily on Dickens' interest in penology in terms of the dichotomy between Dickens' discussion of the subject in fiction and in his journalistic writings. It is Collins' theory that Dickens embodies a more tolerant view of penology in *LD* than he expresses in his journal articles. On Dickens' interest in various forms of incarceration, see Susan Shatto's essay, "Miss Havisham and Mr. Mopes, the Hermit: Dickens and the Mentally Ill," in *Dickens Quarterly,* II, 2 (June, 1985), 43. Shatto states that morbid curiosity motivates Dickens' interest here, but that in the creation of his fiction, Dickens "throws dust in the eyes of the reader," so that the audience dissociates the author from the curiosity seeker. For an historical and psychoanalytical analysis of creativity, see Harry Slochower, *Mythopoesis: Mythic Patterns in the Literary Classics,* (Detroit: Wayne State UP, 1970), p. 12. Slochower notes that with the emergence of nineteenth century technology, creative writers and artists have sustained an image of the self as being incarcerated "in a kind of prison."

[44] *The Letters of Charles Dickens, ed. by His Sister-in-Law/Georgina Hogarth/and His Eldest Daughter/Mamie Dickens/*(London: Chapman and Hall, 1882), III, 171–3. In an earlier letter to Miss Jolly in 1855, Dickens enunciates an important part of his credo for art. He declares, "You write to be read, of course," p. 162.

[45] *Charles Dickens' Uncollected Writings from Household Words: 1850–1859,* ed. Harry Stone (Bloomington: Indiana Univ. Press, 1968), I, 64.

[46] Harvey Peter Sucksmith, *The Narrative Art of Charles Dickens: The Rhetoric of Sympathy and Irony in His Novels* (Oxford: Clarendon, 1970), p. 26. For an earlier text on rhetoric by which an author endeavors to obtrude his imaginary world on the reader, see Wayne Booth, *The Rhetoric of Fiction* (Chicago: Univ. of Chicago Press, 1961).

[47] R. Rupert Roopnaraine, "Time and the Circle in *Little Dorrit,*" *Dickens Studies Annual* (Carbondale: Southern Illinois UP, 1974), 3, 76.

[48] James R. Zimmerman, "Sun and Shadow in *Little Dorrit,*" *The Dickensian,* 83, 2, (Summer 1987) 103. Zimmerman is able to remark on Dickens' nonconventional use of light and dark imagery in *Little Dorrit,* which precludes a "black-and-white" interpretation of the novel.

2

Deception: In Society, Characterization and Narrative Strategy

In various social, psychological and narrative fundamentals, the theme of deceit permeates *Little Dorrit* and surfaces, albeit enigmatically, in plot, characterization and prose style. Dickens' artful presentation of these constituent parts undermines traditional expectations of a Victorian family novel. Fraudulence is shown, in all strata of society, to subvert the individual and the nation.

One of the significant social issues of Dickens' concern, in his eleventh novel, is the state of the nation. Deception, as practised on a national scale, is personified by the fictional bureau called the Circumlocution Office. In the chapter titled "Concerning the Whole Science of Government" Dickens describes this supreme governmental agency as a bureaucratic machine which paralyzes the nation. Instead of expediting and facilitating matters of public concern the Circumlocution Office obstructs and confounds all business transactions with which its office comes in contact. When William Dorrit, who has been immurred in the Marshalsea for almost a quarter of a century, inherits a legacy and endeavors to pay his debts, Lord Decimus of the Circumlocution Office remarks that "it was six months before we knew how to take the money or give a receipt for it" (II, 12, 621).

Dickens indicates that fraudulence is not only the essence of the Circumlocution Office, but that deception operates in all of society's undertakings, and that all of society is imprisoned by its deceptiveness. One of the units of society in which deceit is practiced is represented by the prisoners of the Marshalsea. The collegians, unlike those in the Circumlocution Office, do not engage in unconscionable deceit, but practice deception as a matter of form. Good manners in communication partly require falsehood, and the whole of prison society adapts to the charade. The collegians' pretense to Dorrit is enacted out of both kindness and selfishness—kindness, because it is good form not to intrude on another's delusions, and selfishness because it is easier to placate Dorrit by telling him what he wants to hear than to confront him with the truth. The collegians tend to bow to convention rather than to risk confrontation. On one level some of them accept the image Dorrit projects. They assist in the pious fraud of not letting Dorrit know that Tip is a prisoner, that Fanny is a dancer, that Frederick is a musician and that Amy is a seamstress. These deceptions regarding his family are enacted in order to preserve Dorrit's inflated sense of gentility. Yet behind his back some of the collegians laugh at his pretensions.

The collegians, although deprived of their liberty, are much like the rest of the world. They have their hopes and their fears. They dream of a better life; they are concerned with food and drink, with their families, with news of the larger world. They read the newspapers and have a social life. They give birth. They fall sick and die.

The formal conventions of pretense established by the collegians in their relationship to William Dorrit has as its analogue the formal conventions of pretense established by society, especially in response to Mr. Merdle. Of the latter:

> Admiralty said Mr. Merdle was a wonderful man, Treasury said he was a new power in the country, and would be able to buy up the whole House of Commons.
>
> (I, 21, 295)

Mr. Merdle, a forger and a thief on a national scale, one who has the idiosyncratic habit of grasping his wrists so as to appear to be "taking himself into custody," is no more a wonderful man than is Mr. Dorrit, whose selfishness is a destructive force that retards Amy's growth. Mr. Merdle, "a master of humbug," swindles the nation. Since he understands humankind's insatiable greed, and can deceive people completely, he lures citizens from all walks of life to invest in his bank, which then fails. As a consequence Mr. Merdle commits suicide. He slashes his wrists in the steam baths with a tortoise shell penknife he borrows from Fanny for the purpose. When he asks to borrow the instrument, Fanny, ignorant of his intention, offers him a pearl-handled knife, which he refuses. The ironic inference Dickens is making is that even during the commission of suicide form plays a role. According to Mr. Merdle's idea of appropriate demeanor he would present a more masculine image if his body were discovered with a tortoise shell penknife than with a pearl-handled one.

Dorrit, another master of pretense, instills the fraudulent belief in Amy that he is a good father, but his actions prove otherwise. The copper coins bestowed, by other prisoners, upon his youngsters to ease their impoverished condition are used with Mr. Dorrit's complete acquiescence to provide him with meat and drink. Providing her father with food that should be hers, Amy grows up malnourished. She is so frail in appearance, she looks like a child. Emotionally, Dorrit retards her development by depriving her of her rightful inheritance of childhood. At the age of eight she begins to be aware of his demands on her to attend to his emotional needs. He requires her constant attendance, manipulating her into a life of drudgery:

> even in the matter of lifting and carrying; through how much weariness
> and hopelessness and how many secret tears; she trudged on, until
> recognized as useful, even indispensible.
>
> (I, 7, 111)

At an immature age, in her short-lived childhood, she undertakes numerous adult roles, becoming the fulcrum of the household. Mother to her father, protector to her brother, housekeeper to her sister, she functions as Dorrit's surrogate wife. At thirteen she keeps the family accounts. At twenty-two, when it is time for her to consider her own future, she cleaves to her father, yearning for a reciprocal devotion which his selfishness can not accommmodate. She grows up in the belief that her primary and abiding duty is to her father, and spends her life trying to provide him with material and emotional comforts. She works twelve hours a day to furnish him with sartorial luxuries, while her own clothes remain threadbare and inadequate. Dorrit instills in her the idea of selflessness and she expends her life in devotion to him until his death.

Because of Dorrit's misuse of Amy and because of his fraudulent claims on her time and energy, the reader has a tendency to forget the kind of man Mr. Dorrit is when he first comes to the Marshalsea. Dickens describes him as:

> a shy retiring man . . . with a mild voice . . . and irresolute hands
> . . . which nervously [wander] to his trembling lip a hundred times, in
> the first half-hour of his acquaintance with the jail. His principal anxiety
> [is] about his wife.
>
> (I, 6, 98)

After showing us the portrait of a mild-mannered and helpless middle-aged victim of a bad investment whose intricacies he can neither understand nor from which he can extricate himself (a pawn of an inhumane judicial system), Dickens shows how the passage of time in prison effects an alteration in Dorrit's personality. Incarceration numbs and dehumanizes him. "Crushed at first by his imprisonment he soon found a dull relief in it" (I, 6, 103). And when, accommodating to prison life, Dorrit becomes the Father of the Marshalsea he grows proud, vain and pompous. He affects genteel mannerisms and refuses to acknowledge that his daughters work. When Fanny accepts a job as a dancer Amy feels it is necessary to "go through an elaborate form" of pretense with her father to accommodate to his pretensions. Dickens traces Mr. Dorrit's development from a bewildered debtor to a selfish poseur whose own inadequacies promote deception in his youngest daughter.

The fostering of guile is not limited to the echelons of prison society. Deception is encouraged also by the elite, who must observe certain societal modes of behavior. The female counterpart to male fabrication in society is enacted by Mrs. Gowan with the connivance of Mrs. Merdle. Although Mrs. Gowan will ultimately acquiesce to the marriage of her son to Pet Meagles, she pretends to consider the forthcoming union a demeaning one. According to the observed customs of her class, Mrs. Gowan must engage in a formal ceremony of feigned distress with Mrs. Merdle. Mrs. Merdle, the forger's wife and "High Priestess of Society," will then be so gracious as to bestow her blessings on the nuptials. Accordingly, Mrs. Gowan presents the impending marriage to Mrs. Merdle as an event she has tried her utmost to prevent, but having failed in her efforts, requires Mrs. Merdle's assurance that she is justified in consenting to the unfortunate union. Mrs. Merdle, also acting within the specified form of sham that operates on such occasions, profers her blessings. The "High Priestess of Society" has thus reacted according to convention, playing out the charade of pretended sympathy customary to the situation and has nobly reaffirmed the action that Mrs. Gowan had determined to pursue in advance of their tete-a-tete. Mrs. Gowan knows that Mrs. Merdle has discerned her intentions, as will the rest of Society, but she has performed the deceptive minuet which Society expects and therefore she is satisfied, as Society is gratified, by pretense.

A milder form of artifice distinguishes the locution of Mrs. Plornish. Dickens indicates that duplicity is so much a part of the formal conventions of speech in all strata of society that he uses a negative with the verb "deceive" to describe Mrs. Plornish's method of oral communication. When Arthur Clennam arrives at Bleeding Heart Yard to talk with Mr. Plornish in an effort to gather information that might, in future, be helpful to the Dorrits, he asks if Mr. Plornish is at home. " 'Well, sir,' said Mrs. Plornish . . . 'not to deceive you, he's gone to look for a job!' " Dickens adds that Mrs. Plornish "would deceive you, under any circumstances, as little as might be; but she had a trick of answering in this provisional form." Aside from this odd utterance which clearly characterizes Mrs. Plornish in the reader's mind, Dickens has another motive in depicting her idiosyncratic speech pattern. He is asserting that improbity is ubiquitous, is part of the ritual of social life, and that even as honest a character as Mrs. Plornish will deceive if necessary, albeit as little as possible. He does not say she will never delude under any circumstances, but "as little as might be," and yet we view her as an honest, appealing and worthy character.

Dickens recognizes gradations of ethical values in deceit. There are unscrupulous frauds such as those perpetrated by Mr. Merdle, and there are self-delusions such as those engaged in by Mrs. Plornish. Dickens presents an additional example of Mrs. Plornish's innocuous deception in a visual and historic perspective. Mrs. Plornish, who, in Volume II, becomes the recipient of a little shop-parlor as a result of Dorrit's good fortune, decorates her "Happy Cottage" with scenes from the pastoral past. The visual depiction of pastoral scenes is a fiction in which she rejoices, and in the hierarchy of pretense it is a harmless attempt at self-deception. She has her shop-parlor painted to represent the exterior of a thatched cottage surrounded by blooming flowers and a cloud of pigeons emerging from a pigeon house. For Mrs. Plornish, coming out of the shop and hearing her father singing "Chloe" inside, while she is in the act of observing the exterior of her painted shop, is an evocation of the Golden Age revived (II, 13, 630), in itself a deceptive historical tale of a time when mankind was thought to have lived in a perpetual state of harmony. The illusion Mrs. Plornish has of the Golden Age is a personal fairy tale to which she clings for comfort. As a personal illusion it is harmless, whereas Dorrit's fixed false belief in his own gentility is a delusion that affects everyone with whom he comes into contact, and as such it is harmful, particularly to him and to his youngest daughter.

In this novel of deception, which creates a dismal picture of English society, deceit plays a role in almost all of the characters' lives. Gowan deceives Pet by his questionable charms; Miss Wade misrepresents freedom to Tattycoram; Pancks deludes himself and Arthur with facts and figures; Arthur misleads himself and Doyce about abhorring speculation; Pet tries to persuade herself and Amy that she is happy; Casby masquerades as his tenants' benefactor; Flintwinch is in conspiracy with Mrs. Clennam to suppress knowledge about the Dorrit legacy; Mrs. Clennam deceives her son into believing that she is his natural mother and Rigaud temporarily cheats justice.

Rigaud, a citizen of the world, deceives twelve good Frenchmen and true (a jury of his peers) who acquit him of a murder that Dickens wants us to know he committed. Given the information about Rigaud's cosmopolitan heritage (his Swiss father, his French and English mother, his own Belgian birth) indicates that deception is practised in the world at large. Peter Christmas observes that Rigaud's deceitfulness is part of his intrinsic evil. He states that personal and societal ills in *Little Dorrit* are universal and that evil is not confined to England, but is a world-wide malaise. The widened scope of universal villainy is represented by the scenic action beyond the borders of England. Book I opens in France, with Rigaud in prison, and Book II in Switzerland, embracing the theme of universal wickedness.

Deception in *Little Dorrit* emerges on various thematic levels, indicating that Dickens regards it as an international social evil, integral to social conventions. In his philosophically wide-angled view of the world, Dickens suggests that formal social conventions exist at the expense of honesty and that society paradoxically requires subterfuge for its existence. In *Little Dorrit* Dickens creates a realistic portrait of mankind in which the hierarchy of conventions allows for varying forms and degrees of deceit, some of which are individual and harmless whereas others threaten the public welfare.

In his delineation of character, Dickens insinuates the notion that self-delusion disables the self-deluded. Some of the consequences of self-deception are shown in the prevailing disorders of the following characters: the arrested development of Amy and Arthur, the mental collapse of William Dorrit, the paralysis of Mrs. Clennam and the suicide of Mr. Merdle.

Stephen Marcus comments in *Dickens: From Pickwick to Dombey* (1965), that one of Dickens' chief concerns in *Little Dorrit* is the connection between social and personal disorders.

Aside from stratagems in plot, guile plays a significant role in characterization, of which the novel's heroine is a grave illustration. Amy's prison birth is a sociological factor in her meager opportunity for a life of fulfillment, and her warped childhood is a psychological factor in her devious and complex personality. She is self-deceptive and she deceives others. She deludes herself, in part, about her father and her relationship to him, and she misleads various segments of society with an image of her angelic purity. She is somewhat less successful in totally deceiving her family.

A child of the Marshalsea, Amy is reared, not by the Father of the Marshalsea, but by her godfather, the turnkey on the lock. Bob is her constant companion, providing her with the only nurture she receives. His store of toys and tales and his excursions with her to the pastoral countryside, are her only acquaintance with the world beyond the spiked walls of the Marshalsea. She exists in this semblance of childhood until she attains the age of eight, when her father becomes a widower and Amy becomes an adult. At eight she assumes the role of ministering angel to her family in general and to her father in particular. She deserts her livelier place at the turnkey's side and takes her post beside her father, observing him with pitying and protective glances. Her love and devotion are described as "the inspiration of a poet or a priest." But such selflessness is not without its destructive feature for Amy, to which Dickens alerts us in the paragraph immediately following that which depicts Amy's inspired labors. Born and bred in a false social condition:

> drinking from infancy of a well whose waters had their own peculiar stain, their unwholesome and unnatural taste; the Child of the Marshalsea began her womanly life.
>
> (I, 7, 111)

In the years from eight to thirteen, Amy becomes indispensable to the Dorrit menage, assuming full responsibility for her pretentious father, her wayward sister, and her idle brother. In taking on a premature matriarchal burden, subterfuge becomes a way of life for Amy. Deceit in Little Dorrit functions as a survival mechanism, enabling her to wield the power she needs to overcome the despairing drudgery and unwholesome condition of her life. Turning fact into fiction, she initiates and preserves the lie that her brother continues to be, as is she, a voluntary inhabitant of the Marshalsea. The fiction is not composed by Tip; it is Amy's idea and Tip yields to her desire to shield her father from truth. When Tip reveals to Arthur that he is a prisoner he says, " 'My sister has a theory that our governor must never know it. I don't see why, myself' " (I, 8, 127).

Amy's belief that to expose Mr. Dorrit to the truth "would kill their father if he ever knew it" serves an important function in her life. It provides her with some control of her environment. If the fabric of deception that has been woven into so many areas of her life were to disintegrate, her capacity for coping would diminish, and she would no longer be the mainstay of the family. By plotting and planning secretively she controls her world, to a degree. She is the general of the Dorrit family (until the arrival of Mrs. General). Mr. Dorrit is merely the family's figurehead. Amy needs to dominate the environment to the best of her confined ability in order to perpetuate her sense of purpose. She has concentrated all her efforts on basic survival and on pleasing her father. To be a dutiful daughter means, in part, to acquiesce. She cannot be open and direct. She must be submissive and seemingly passive, and therefore she resorts to indirect ways of acting. Being deceptive is part of a pattern of behavior which enables her to be of value to the family. As she tells Clennam, " 'I could never have been of any use if I had not pretended a little' " (I, 14, 211).

Although the subterfuges Amy practices purport, in part, to be enacted out of love, they perpetuate Dorrit's infantile attitude. By encouraging Mr. Dorrit's pretentiousness, Amy corroborates and reinforces his unsuitable behavior. In so doing she is herself engaged in deception since she knows he is being inappropriate. We tend to overlook her deceits since they operate under the guise of love, within the spirit of her realistically painful drudgery. Dickens' point is that, taking into account Amy's situation, her deceptions, while not laudable, are understandable.

Amy knows that deceptiveness is not commendable and is occasionally discomfited by her own behavior. When Arthur follows her to the Marshalsea and intrudes upon her in Dorrit's cell, he discovers the motive for her feigned preference to dine alone in his mother's house. The subterfuge she enacted is rooted in, and centers on, her relationship with her father:

> She had brought the meat home [from Mrs. Clennam's] that she should
> have eaten herself. . . . She started, colored deeply, and turned white.
>
> (I, 8, 121)

Startled at having been caught, reddening from the heat of shame, and blanching in fear are responses that elicit an examination of impulses. Ostensibly the act of denying herself nourishment in order to feed her father can be viewed as admirable. Why does it produce discomfort, humiliation and fear? It does so due to an element of inappropriateness in the dimension of her attentiveness to her father. Amy, who functions in Mrs. Clennam's house as a retiring seamstress, one who hides in shadows, officiates in prison as a wife and mother. A hidden and unnatural aspect of her personality has thus been unintentionally revealed to Arthur, a comparative stranger. Subconsciously, if not cognitively, Amy is aware that to minister to her father as though she were his wife is unfitting, but it is a role she desperately wants. To be close to her father in an intimate relationship, to be needed by him, to care for him and have him to herself are the psychological motivations for her drudgery and deception.

Amy's self-delusion that Mr. Dorrit must be protected from truth, that the knowledge of truth would kill him, is an exaggeration inconsistent with reality. Mr. Dorrit would have survived the knowledge of Tip's incarceration, as he endured his own imprisonment and as he coped with the death of his wife, at which time he "remained shut up in his room for a fortnight. . . . But he got pretty well over it in a month or two" (I, 6, 104). Mr. Dorrit survives adversity very well; he does not survive success. More than a score of years in prison do not provide him with the ability to adjust to freedom. He exists in prison on the fiction of emancipation, on the dim, almost forgotten hope of liberty. In the actuality of release, he does not prosper. He disintegrates mentally and dies prematurely when liberated. He can adapt to imprisonment; he cannot contend with freedom.

Dorrit's mishandling of liberty is a particularization of the national condition, which is represented by the Circumlocution Office. Both Dorrit and the Circumlocution Office spend money foolishly, Dorrit for a retinue of servants, the Circumlocution Office for a retinue of Barnacles. Both Dorrit and the Circumlocution Office are interested in the superficial forms and conventions of society. They are alike more concerned with style than with substance. Both Dorrit and the Circumlocution Office have the money and the freedom to misuse their power and to treat others in an abusive manner. Both Dorrit and the Circumlocution Office are spiritually imprisoning themselves by their mismanagement of power, money and liberty.

In *Little Dorrit* Dickens is saying that England is one vast Marshalsea, that the nation is undermining efforts aimed at societal improvement and that the very forms and conventions of society are imprisoning. Dickens indicates that not only does a connection exist between personal and national misuse of liberty, but that in addition, a connection exists between the Marshalsea, which is a microcosmic representation of society, and the Circumlocution Office, which is the personification of the nation. Both institutions paralyze. The Circumlocution Office immobilizes the nation; the Marshalsea benumbs the prisoners. The former debases individuals by its disregard of their needs and capabilities; the latter dehumanizes prisoners by its indifference to human potential. The two institutions restrict liberty and deny the pursuit of happiness. Both institutions preserve the system; the Circumlocution Office perpetuates power and the Marshalsea perpetuates poverty. The illogical procedures which operate in the Circumlocution Office reflect the senseless policies which function in the Marshalsea. In *Dickens The Novelist* (1970), the Leavises observe that once debtors are imprisoned for non-payment of debt, they have no means of amassing the funds necessary to cancel their obligations. Indefinite prison sentences preclude the debtor's ability ever to pay off his debts. Thus the illogic of incarceration until a debt is repaid guarantees that the debt will never be paid, and ensures the debtor's continuing poverty. Debtors are segregated by an inhumane judicial system as citizens are sequestered by a harsh political structure.

An example of a citizen who becomes the victim of an inhumane political system and the illogical policy of the Circumlocution Office is shown by Dickens' portrait of the inventor, Daniel Doyce. Doyce represents the skill and ingenuity which, if recognized by England, would permit positive progress for the nation. But the nation, represented by the Circumlocution Office, gives no credence or support to Doyce's efforts. It resists his attempts at societal improvement, and by its machinations refuses to issue him a patent for his invention. Doyce is a victim of a callous political system, as Dorrit is a victim of an unfeeling judicial system. However, a characteristic difference exists between the two men. Dorrit is a weak man who is incarcerated for almost a quarter of a century for a bankruptcy which no one (including the Circumlocution Office) can disentangle. Dorrit, who is bowed down by his imprisonment, quickly adapts to it and finds life a quieter refuge than it had been before. "He was under lock and key; but the lock and key that kept him in, kept numbers of his troubles out" (I, 6, 103). Doyce however, has a stronger will than Dorrit. Doyce possesses the stamina, determination, and sense of self-worth to overcome the obstacles put in his way by the system. After years of harassment by the Circumlocution

Office Doyce eventually takes his invention abroad to assure its manufacture and success. Therefore another country becomes the beneficiary of his invention, while the Circumlocution Office has lost the opportunity of utilizing the resourcefulness of a talented citizen for the benefit of England.

Doyce, unlike Dorrit, uses his freedom with efficacy. But Doyce's partner, Clennam, is another example of a character who misgoverns his liberty. Like Dorrit, Arthur is limited, in that he too is unable to deal with the responsibility that comes with release. Although he is able to cope with financial confinement, he is unable to contend with fiscal freedom. While he is working under his father's aegis abroad, he functions with honesty and propriety. Once he removes himself from parental protectorship he cannot handle the pressures of license. He is given financial freedom by his partner, but he, like Dorrit, abuses the authority vested in him. Although he promises Doyce that he will not speculate, Arthur gambles with his partner's funds, deluding himself with the rationalization that everbody else is investing in Merdle's Bank, including cautious people, like Pancks, and that therefore it cannot be a wager. His disavowal of his dishonorable behavior precipitates an act of deceit that ultimately results in his incarceration in the Marshalsea Debtor's Prison. In his denial of truth, Arthur mirrors the actions of numerous characters in *Little Dorrit*, and exhibits the self-delusory inclination of his creator, Dickens.

The malady of self-deception which is manifest in the hero surfaces in yet another form in the heroine. Amy's self-delusion functions as a denial of reality which occasionally minimizes her painful existence and makes life more bearable for her than objective truth would. Dickens offers two examples of self-deception which operate in Amy in similar fashion and both illustrations concentrate on her unwholesome relationship to her father, William Dorrit. Amy has come to Arthur's lodgings to thank him for his generosity in having Tip released from prison. It is a bitterly cold night when she arrives and Arthur lights the fire for her, observing that her feet are frozen in their worn shoes:

Little Dorrit was not ashamed of her poor shoes. . . . Little Dorrit had
a misgiving that he might blame her father . . . that he might think
'why did he dine to-day, and leave this little creature to the mercy of
the cold stones!' She had no belief that it would have been a just
reflection; she simply knew, by experience, that such delusions did
sometimes present themselves to people.

(I, 14, 209)

Amy is aware that she is a drudge, that she works to provide
her father with sartorial luxuries while her own shoes do not
protect her against the elements. Such awareness must be
repressed in order to avert despair. The truth of her condition
would be unsupportable otherwise. She must maintain a
fantasy about Dorrit's love and devotion which anyone's diminution of would destroy. Any incursion on her belief in her
father's worthiness diminishes her sense of purpose and places
it in jeopardy. How can she go on sacrificing her life for her
father if society questions his moral right to receive her sacrifice? If, as is intimated, Dorrit should not permit her to walk
about ill-shod, then her sacrifice is in vain. In order to give
meaning to her purpose in life, which is to provide for and
protect Dorrit, she must delude herself regarding his selfishness. Therefore she is especially sensitive to any remark which
might be construed as minimizing Dorrit's love for her. She
must deny the reality of his selfishness in order to carry on.

Amy's tendency toward denial of reality is also shown in a
later dialogue between the Dorrit sisters during the wealthy
period of their lives. Fanny has revealed her awareness of Mrs.
General's designs on William Dorrit, and the latter's reciprocal
interest. Amy's response is, on the surface, one of cautious
placidity. She says, " 'At least you may be mistaken, Fanny.
Now may you not?' " Fanny's retort is shrewd and perceptive.
" 'O yes I may be . . . but I am not. However, I am glad you
can contemplate such an escape' " (II, 7, 559). Fanny is aware
that Amy's response is a compromise with truth. Amy denies
the validity of Fanny's remarks since acknowledgement would
cause too much pain. If she did not deny the actuality of the
situation she would have to confront the possibility of another

woman usurping her place. Therefore she deludes herself with the seemingly objective response that Fanny must be wrong in her interpretation of the interactions between Mr. Dorrit and Mrs. General.

Although Amy blinds herself to Mrs. General's wiliness, she is very perceptive in assessing treachery in Rigaud. She correctly suspects that Rigaud has poisoned Henry Gowan's dog, and she accurately interprets Rigaud's manner to her as indication of his having secret knowledge about her. She doesn't know what that information might be, but her intuition is later borne out by Rigaud's possession of documents revealing her status as an heiress. The difference between Amy's objectivity regarding Rigaud and her lack of objectivity in regard to her father and Mrs. General lies in the relationship she has with her father. Amy loses perspective where her father is concerned. She cannot view Dorrit with the keen insights with which she readily perceives Rigaud. To do so would destroy her fantasy of becoming a cherished person to her father. If she were to accept the obvious relationship that exists between Mr. Dorrit and Mrs. General, she would have to acknowledge the probability that as Mrs. General's future step-daughter, she would most likely find herself more marginal in her father's affections than heretofore. Therefore, she dare not admit the truth. In Dickens' bifocal view of Amy, he presents her delusion as a personal malady, and paradoxically intimates that her defensiveness against reality operates as a survival mechanism that allows her to accept her wretched existence.

In the service of characterization, Dickens' carefully planned deceptions are integral to his narrative strategies in *Little Dorrit*. One of the author's misleading techniques is to betray the reader into believing that Amy personifies many of the standard Victorian virtues, which in fact she does. However, since she is also essentially a human and complex character, Dickens invests her personality with unpleasant traits as well, which he points to more obliquely than he does to her good qualities. The reason for his equivocal depiction of Amy is that he wants to present her realistically, as an impure heroine, but does not want to dissuade the reader from empathizing with her. Therefore he disguises her unlikable characteristics beneath a saintly exterior.

In an important chapter titled "Little Dorrit's Party," Dickens reveals the subtlety of his strategy through the actions and dialogue of his protagonist. After Little Dorrit has thanked Arthur for having had Tip released from prison, she assures Arthur that she and Maggy have lodgings for the night. Subsequently, the two girls depart. It is after midnight as they traverse the London streets. Some distance from Arthur's rooms, Amy stops at a doorway, cautions Maggy to be silent, and makes a show of rapping softly on a stranger's door. Then she listens. Hearing no sound from inside, she says to Maggy:

> 'Now this is a good lodging for you Maggy, and we must not give offence. Consequently, we will knock only twice, and not very loud; and if we cannot wake them so, we must walk about till day.'
>
> (I, 14, 216)

For whom is Amy enacting this charade? For Maggy? Why should she dissemble to the poor grotesque? Is pretense so essential an element of Amy's being that she does it without cause? Is this a motiveless act? Although Amy's ruse appears unmotivated, the action serves a purpose. It is part of Dickens' deceptive narrative strategy. He renders an ostensibly groundless act, then glosses it over with a rationale, obscuring the dubiousness of the motive in the rationale. Only by thinking hard about the uncertain act can we arrive at what Dickens is actually saying about his protagonist.

In "deceptive" language, then, Dickens is trying to show that Amy is not a pure heroine, that she may not even be a very likable character, and that she is a negative example of purity. For what other reason would he have Amy rapping at the door of a house softly, pretending she's expected, knowing that she's not, and furthermore, not intending to have her knock heard? Why this deception? To what purpose, but to show an act of cruelty on Amy's part? The unkindness lies in the inspiration of hope held out to Maggy for a place to spend the night, when Little Dorrit has no intention of attempting to ask for shelter. The disappointment engendered in Maggy is qualitatively greater than if no hope had been initially offered. It is a wilfull act to a helpless unfortunate, one who is less favorably endowed than Amy, and certainly one who is almost totally dependent on Amy's good will. Dickens is showing that Maggy is Amy's scapegoat (as Amy is her family's scapegoat). Dickens is correctly observing that to be victimized and to victimize in return is part of the psychological human condition. This unheroic aspect of Amy's personality is revealed to show how a character who is dehumanized by her environment cannot realistically be expected to behave angelically in all situations.

If Dickens wanted to create Amy as a purely positive example of purity, he would have restructured two incidents in the scene. He would not have had Amy hold out false hope to Maggy, and he would have had her say initially what she says eventually, which is: " 'Maggy, we must do the best we can, my dear. We must be patient and wait for day.' " (I, 14, 216). In addition, he would not have followed one unheroic act with another, unless he were intent on the reader's perceiving subliminally that Amy has her own personal disorders. He would not include a gross sexual image of Little Dorrit kissing the bar of the Marshalsea gate, a symbolically incestuous gesture, saying of her father, " 'I hope he is sound asleep . . . and does not miss me' " (I, 14, 216). Considered cumulatively, the juxtaposition of the subtly compassionless act and the incestuous one add to the sense the reader has of Amy's inappropriate and impure behavior in this chapter.

A further instance of the deceptive technique of Dickens' narrative strategy is shown in the manner in which he combines filial duty with sexuality, glossing the latter with the former. Dickens lets the reader know that Amy has incestuous impulses through the voice of a minor character, Mrs. Chivery. Mrs. Chivery's words may easily be forgotten, but if remembered, they add to a comprehensive picture of Amy's hidden feelings. Mrs. Chivery's analysis of the unnatural bond between Amy and Dorrit is founded on a correct premise. When

Amy rejects Young John Chivery his mother explains Amy's motive. She says that Mr. Dorrit refuses to share his daughter with anyone and that Amy agrees with Mr. Dorrit's possessiveness, and that furthermore, Amy herself has no intention of ever becoming anybody's wife (I, 22, 304).

The grossest example of Amy's incestuous yearning is the one which shows her kissing the bar of the Marshalsea gate. However, there are other more subtle examples of her interactions with her father in which she appears to be responding with filial obedience, yet her verbal responses to him are not entirely suitable to a father-daughter relationship. Interspersed throughout the novel there are fragments of conversation which are reminiscent of conversations a married couple might be expected to engage in:

> Dorrit: 'My love you have had a life of hardship here.'
> Amy: 'Don't think of that, dear, I never do.'   (I, 19, 275)
> Amy: 'I would not wilfully bring a tear to your eyes, dear love.'
>   (I, 31, 420)
> Amy: 'Hush, hush my own dear! Kiss me!'   (II, 5, 533)
> Amy: 'Dear father, loved father, darling of my heart.'   (I, 19, 272)
> Amy: 'Look at me father, kiss me father, only think of me father, for
>   one little moment.'   (I, 19, 273)

In addition to her phraseology, some of Amy's actions, while those of a dutiful, devoted daughter, leave no doubt as to their deeper symbolic significance. Describing the ambiguous filial-sexual quality in Amy's character, Dickens writes:

> She never left him all that night, as if she had done him a wrong which her tenderness would hardly repair. She sat by him in his sleep, at times softly kissing him with suspended breath and calling him in a whisper by some endearing name.
>
>   (I, 19, 276)

The words Dickens uses to describe her reactions to Dorrit are: "Poor dear, good dear, kindest, dearest," and when Dorrit suggests to Amy that the time is not too far distant to consider marriage for her, Amy replies:

'Oh no! Let me stay with you. I beg and pray that I may stay with you!
I want nothing but to stay and take care of you.'

(II, 15, 669)

It is interesting to note the rare occasions on which Amy
responds openly with a lack of compliance. They relate to
situations in which her father wants to offer her to another
man. An instance of Amy's disobedience to Dorrit's wishes is
her rejection of Young John Chivery. It is to Amy's credit that
she does not accede to William's objectionable proposal to
accept Young John's attentions, but her antipathy to and
refusal of Young Chivery are due to the fact that she is
engrossed in, and overwhelmed by her feelings, both filial and
sexual, for her father. She is depicted as combining repressed
sexuality and Victorian virtue. Her suppressed sexual impulse
binds her to her father and her Victorian morality glosses her
sexual urge so that what is most noticeable seems most pious.
Her undutiful act of rejecting Young John has as its primary
motivation her feelings of yearning for her father. Although
Dorrit wants her to himself he is not averse to parcelling out her
attentions to Young Chivery if he thinks it to his advantage.
The situation into which he wishes to propel her with Young
John is an insupportable one to Amy. Her father wants her to
accept the attentions of a young man to whom she has an
aversion. Dorrit suggests that she accommodate herself to
Young John, to "lead him on," as a dutiful servant to her
father. Describing his reliance on the good will of the turnkey
as essential to his well being, William indicates that Amy has
given offense to Young John, and by extension, to John's
father, for refusing her suitor's attentions. With emotional
abandon, William attempts to evoke guilt in her for so doing.
He is aware that his proposal for Amy to encourage John is
mortifying to both of them, but selfishness urges him on:

'It's impossible to forget . . . that in such a life as mine, I am unfortu-
nately dependent on these men for something, every hour of the
day.'. . . While he spoke, he was opening and shutting his hands like
valves; so conscious all the time of that touch of shame, that he shrunk
before his own knowledge of his meaning.

(I, 19, 270–1)

Although his statement contains an element of truth, the moral force of decent behavior is being subverted, and Dorrit knows it. That is why he digresses to maudlin self pity, which is an effort to deceive both himself and his daughter of the state of degradation into which he has fallen. While he is acknowledging that he is a "squalid disgraced wretch," articulating his condition is a sanction to provoke increased guilt in Amy and to persuade her of the efficacy of his proposal.

In further attempts to influence her, he refers to his impending death. His allusions to dying are intended to instill terror in his daughter at the thought of losing him. By arousing this painful emotion in Amy, Dorrit hopes to becloud the issue of his responsibility for his indecent behavior.

Indecency and death are linked in the scene. The diminution of decency is a moral decay, and the breaking down of civilized form and behavior in this episode foreshadows the symbolic acting out of the incestuous wish between father and daughter which occurs during the last ten days of Dorrit's life. Amy tends him, and whereas he has shut out the rest of the world, Amy is never out of his thoughts or sight. He "had constant need of her, and could not turn without her." She is so worn with fatigue from tending him that they occasionally "would slumber together." Dickens has invested the deathbed scene with the unrealized and unresolved incestuous yearnings of both father and daughter, but the reader is unlikely to take into account the subliminal sexuality to which Dickens is alluding because of the show of filial duty in Amy's behavior, in addition to an aspect of virtue, which plays its role in her tender care of her dying father.

Covert sexuality functions in another bedroom scene (between Fanny and Frederick) but the interaction of uncle and niece has a different tone from the interplay between father and daughter. Dickens cites an example of the possibility of incest to which Fanny is subjected. In creating this episode for Fanny, Dickens emphasizes the contrast between her response and Amy's. In the action between Fanny and Frederick, Dickens depicts Fanny in one of her usual abrasive moods, but her sharpness is motivated by an underlying danger inherent in the situation. Fanny is living with Frederick in mean cramped quarters where minimal privacy obtains. When Frederick wants to fetch her he goes to the bedroom door to open it. He does not knock. Fanny holds the door closed from within but that does not deter Frederick from attempting to open it. He succeeds to the degree that portions of Fanny's undergarments are seen through the open door and he desists only after Fanny has reprimanded him with the command, "Don't, stupid!" Fanny, unlike Amy, does not seek intimate associations with either her uncle or her father. She recognizes Frederick's inappropriate action and reacts accordingly with suitable impatience, albeit with a sharp retort. If the possibility of sexual danger were not so disturbing to Fanny she would have used a milder form of reproach to her uncle.

Dickens' depiction of Fanny is an additional example of his deceptive narrative strategy. To a great degree Fanny speaks truth, but Dickens glosses the validity of her remarks by couching them in wrathful language. So that whereas he pretends to present an unadulterated portrait of an explosive and exploitive character, he is really using Fanny as an accurate voice to expose Amy's irksome characteristics. Because of Dickens' deceptive prose there is a tendency on the part of the reader to dismiss Fanny as a pretentious, vengeful and wayward young woman. These unheroic traits are assuredly aspects of her personality, but the perspicacity of her acerbic remarks about her younger sister deserve consideration.

When Fanny accepts a bracelet from Mrs. Merdle to stop seeing her son Sparkler, Amy is dismayed that Fanny would accept a bribe. Fanny's defense of her unsavory act reveals a rankling truth about the sisters' relationship:

> 'If you despise me,' she said in tears, 'for being a dancer, why did you put me in the way of being one? It was your doing.'
>
> (I, 20, 290)

Although it was, in part, a virtuous act for Amy to prepare her sister for a livelihood by arranging for Fanny to become a

dancer, Amy was establishing her sister in a tawdry occupation. Little Dorrit contracted for herself to learn the art of
needlework, a respectable occupation, and one that would
keep her home in the evenings. Additionally, it was Little
Dorrit who planned for Fanny to live with Uncle Frederick. In
sending Fanny out of the Marshalsea to live with their uncle,
Amy was successfully eliminating the other female in the
house. Fanny could have easily kept her job while continuing
to live in the family's prison home. Ostensibly, living with
Uncle Frederick would eliminate the need for Fanny to explain
to her father how she was earning her livelihood. However,
Fanny was not so timid that she would not have ventured forth
despite Dorrit's objections. By evicting Fanny from her rightful
abode, Amy became the sole woman in Dorrit's life.

When, occasionally, Fanny visits the jail, she does so to
retrieve the clothes Amy has washed and mended for her. By
accepting domestic drudgery from her sister, Little Dorrit is
compensating Fanny for exiling her from the Marshalsea.
Furthermore, domesticity places Amy in the symbolic position
of the connubial role which satisfies her incestuous yearnings.
Dickens is showing that Amy's acts are not clear-cut nor simply
motivated by the need for Fanny to support herself. He is
describing, in misleading prose, the combination of intricacies
which operate in the psyche to produce a purportedly trans-
parent act, but one which is actually opaque.

Fanny is again a perceptive judge of what appears, on the
surface, to be a charitable act that Amy performs, but which is,
additionally, an expression of hostility toward their father.
Amy's hidden motive for the kind deed is exposed by the lie
she tells her father when he confronts her with having been
seen in public, walking arm in arm with Nandy, the pauper.
Amy's neighborliness has been observed by Fanny, who rep-
rimands her for thus disgracing the family.

Since Fanny's pretensions reflect those of Mr. Dorrit, Amy
might have known that her father would consider her action an
assault on his dignity. Both Fanny and Dorrit continually harp
on the distance to be observed between themselves and people

whom they consider to be of inferior status. Being at least subliminally cognizant of this fact, it is a subtle act of hostility on Amy's part to disregard her father's wishes, despite his pretentious motives. When Amy is scolded by Fanny, Amy's response is allegedly a justifiable defense for a gentle act. She says to Fanny " 'Does it disgrace anybody . . . to take care of this old man?' " However, when her father disapproves, Amy cries for forgiveness and pretends ignorance of having done anything to offend. She doesn't defend her action on grounds of compassion for Mr. Nandy as she did with Fanny; instead she says, " 'Tell me how it is, that I may not do it again.' " Enraged at Amy's deceit, Fanny says:

> 'How is it, you prevaricating little piece of goods! . . . You know how it is. I have told you already, so don't fly in the face of Providence by attempting to deny it.'
>
> (I, 31, 419)

Only moments before, Amy had responded to Fanny's disapproval with a justification of her gracious behavior to Mr. Nandy. If she had been telling her father the truth (as Fanny proved she had not) and, if walking arm in arm with a pauper had been motivated primarily by compassion, Amy would have repeated to her father the remark she made to her sister, that it was no disgrace to care for an old man. However, she does not defend her behavior to her father. Instead, she asserts that if she had known that Dorrit would take her action amiss, she would not have taken a stroll with the elderly pauper.

An activity that seems on the surface to have been a merciful endeavor, is actually one motivated by contradictory impulses, including Amy's repressed hostility to Dorrit and her simultaneous yearning for approval from him. That which appears purely virtuous is merely an image of piousness. Amy's pretense of saintliness is, though more subtle, somewhat equivalent to a form of pretentiousness, similar in its element of hypocrisy to Dorrit's. William's affectation is overt; Amy's is covert. As Dorrit's pretension is to gentility, so Amy's implied claim is to purity. She pretends to be morally upright, yet she would forgo a humane act to curry favor with her father. Whereas Dorrit's facade of refinement is a form of self-aggrandizement, the image of virtue that Amy seeks to project is a misguided attempt to secure love. Although differing in motivation, method and degree, the actions of both father and daughter enhance one of the novel's overriding themes, that of hypocrisy.

In another example of artful prose, Dickens indirectly reveals how Amy's dissembling manner functions to goad Fanny's rage. Fanny is ambivalant about her engagement to Edmund Sparkler. She and her sister have discussed the impending marriage on numerous occasions, and Amy is aware of Fanny's dilemma. When Fanny returns home one evening after a dull night with Sparkler, her vexed tone and agitated demeanor signify that she is, once again, vainly attempting to find a satisfactory solution to her self-imposed predicament. She is torn between her disdain of Sparkler and her vengeful desire to thwart his mother by marrying him.

Feigning ignorance of Fanny's consuming concern, Amy asks to know the cause of her sister's distress, a dissembling inquiry that infuriates Fanny who, in turn, calls Little Dorrit a "prevaricating and blind little mole." Her younger sister immediately counters with a patient response. " 'Is it Mr. Sparkler, dear?' "

Amy's mild mannered and affectionate-sounding answer derives from numerous negative impulses and works on various levels. It simulates a mistaken refinement, one that precludes the hearing of a sister's discourteous remarks, which guarantees the repetition of similar abuses. It purports to do so but does not actually address Fanny's troubled soul; instead it ignores prior confidences about Fanny's dichotomous emotions. In addition, Amy's question indicates that she has been cognizant of the cause of her sister's disquiet since the inception of the evening's dialogue, but has elected to play-act in a charade that does not admit of such common considerations of marriage which are alienating Fanny from herself and her sister. Ultimately the charade points to Amy's need to continue to stimulate a behavior pattern that positions her as the focus of Fanny's verbal abuse, even during the period of their lives when they are no longer immured in the Marshalsea.

In the destructive exchange between the siblings, Dickens illustrates the enduring power of ingrained maladaptive behavior. He is depicting a mode of habituated reciprocal acts which obviate the sisters' ability to enjoy mutual acceptance. Although the Dorrits' altered circumstances might be expected to engender a measure of harmony, Dickens strongly suggests that the unwholesome history of the Dorrit sisters constitutes a barrier to change.

Fanny is perceptive about her sister. Amy is not the saintly person she affects to be and her false piety is an irritant and is so described by her older sister. When Fanny pierces the pseudo-saintliness, she reveals the reason that Amy's martyrdom is so irksome. Fanny correctly assesses their interactions in a futile effort to effectuate a change between them. She says of herself that when she makes herself hateful, the best action that Amy could take would be to tell Fanny that she's being odious, but that Amy never confronts her. Instead, by her silent acceptance she tempts and goads Fanny into further obnoxious behavior, and that furthermore the art of Amy's acquiescence is that Fanny frequently finds herself in the position of being forgiven by her younger sibling.

Fanny is enunciating an important facet of reciprocity. She is asking her sister to help her to become a kind and gracious person by confronting her with her inappropriate behavior when it occurs. Although Fanny is enraged with herself for her lack of restraint, she is also angry with Amy for her silent participation which does not resolve their difficult situation but serves to exacerbate it. Fanny, for all her pretentiousness and upward striving toward superficialities, wants to be a better individual than she is. She also desires to modify the pattern of interaction between herself and her sister. However, Amy is, to a degree, content with her martyrdom and does not wish to alter the status quo.

Psychologically, Amy's mode of behavior is understandable.

She cannot compete with her sister's direct and spontaneous outpouring of feelings. She is accustomed to abuse and she accepts it with a show of obedience. She affects the image of a martyr, which in part she is, and in so doing enrages Fanny who sees through the angelic pose to the negative characteristics beneath. These hidden aspects of dissembling, toadying and goading in Amy's personality do not diminish her positive qualities of industriousness, concern and love which function to support and maintain the Dorrit family. Her hidden traits are considered and attended to here as an amplification of a complex character whose social and psychological condition combine to create an intricate, complicated and deceptive personality.

Ever mindful of his readers, Dickens presents Fanny's unheroic traits overtly and forcefully; however, since Little Dorrit is his acknowledged protagonist, he must divulge her unlikeable qualities in discreet fashion. Therefore, he reveals portions of Amy's negative attributes through Fanny's wrathful dialogue. Dickens' technique of indirection and misdirection in characterization is a superb manifestation of his versatility in yielding significant information to an attentive and alert audience.

3

Hostility: In Various Disguises

The manifestation of ill will, which Dickens sees as a pervasive human force, is intrinsic to *Little Dorrit*. A spirit of overt and covert antagonism infuses the novel. Hostility as a mode of interaction emerges on all levels of society. On a national scale it appears in the perversity of the Circumlocution Office; in the social sphere it emerges in the tribal chauvinism of the Bleeding Heart Yarders. Enmity among the characters expresses various kinds and gradations of belligerence, from the savage explosions of William Dorrit to the cold vindictiveness of Mrs. Clennam. Part of the grimness of the novel is due to the animosity in most of the characters' relationships. With the few exceptions of Doyce, Cavalletto and the Plornishes, major and minor characters interweave belligerently. It is the pervasiveness of these hostile interactions which accounts for so much adverse reader reaction to *Little Dorrit*.

A Deceptive Presentation of Flora Finching

One of the most hilarious presentations of hostility appears in the circumlocutory speech patterns of tender-hearted Flora Finching. Flora, a garrulous middle-aged woman, is amiable, sympathetic and romantic. Nonetheless there is an undercurrent of mild antagonism in her dialogue, which is glossed over by her dizzying leaps from one topic to another. Her persistently expressed rancor is motivated by pain. She has been jilted by Arthur and cannot forget it. She alludes to the past, and, by implication, to his rejection of her in almost every conversation. It is the shame and pain of that humiliating memory which causes her to berate him when she says, " 'I might have been dead and buried twenty distinct times over before you had genuinely remembered me.' " She calls him the "insincerest of creatures." She admonishes him for not having written and makes the point that he returned the celebrated eighteenth-century romance *Paul and Virginia* to her "without note or comment," and she adds that had he but sent her a sign she would have followed him to China:

> 'if it had only come back with a red wafer on the cover I should have known that it meant Come to Pekin Nankeen and what's the third place barefoot?'
>
> (I, 13, 195)

Extravagant as her fancy is, implicit in her reproach is the information that she would have defied her father for him. Why hadn't he defied his mother for her?

Arthur gently remonstrates with her, saying that they were both too young and too dependent to do anything other than to accept their separation, but he has invited her reproaches by his inconsiderate behavior. A note or sign, sent to her between the leaves of the romance, would have been a suitable act. Returning the book without a word was a more offensive deed than keeping it would have been. Sending it back signified that he wanted neither memory nor keepsake of their love. Custom decreed that he restore the romance to her, but custom did not decree that he return it without a word of regret.

Arthur's lack of consideration for Flora may have been motivated by his pain at having lost her, but it is also complicated by a pattern he establishes with his first romantic interest and which continues with all his romantic involvements to the end of the novel. He retreats from the fray. As a young man he doesn't fight for Flora; in middle age he won't do battle for Pet; nor will he marry Amy until she, in effect, proposes to him. Whereas in his youth he had "ardently loved" Flora, after their engagement was broken he dismissed her from his mind "as if she had been dead." Perhaps the only way he knew how to survive the loss of his first love was to deny it, and Flora's existence.

However, from Flora's perspective Arthur's silence was unwarranted. She had been led to believe that he loved her and some word of remorse or pained acceptance of the separation would have indicated a minimal concern for her despair. He made no attempt to comfort her in some small measure, and it is his disregard for the emotional amenities as well as for the social amenities that causes her, on his return, to make reference to his lack of consideration for her, and to continually berate him.

One of the reasons we tend to ignore this rankling element in Flora's conversation is that Dickens presents it deceptively. It is set forth, indirectly, as a manifestation of Flora's idiosyncratic speech pattern, and is therefore easily disregarded, particularly since her chatter is so ludicrous. Telescoping time and events, Flora inserts what seem like non-sequiturs in her kaleidoscopic discourse, except that these non-sequiturs are really the crux of her conversation. She pursues one topic after another with such extraordinary speed that the reader is overwhelmed by fleeting stimuli. Flora vents her hurt feelings in reproach to Arthur, and then immediately retreats from the utterance. She withdraws lest her rebuke seem too harsh. Typically complaining about the past with great rapidity and confusing leaps of thought, she refers to a time, twenty years before, when parental interference wrecked their marriage plans:

> 'when they severed the golden bond that bound us and threw us into fits of crying on the sofa nearly choked at least myself everything was changed and in giving my hand to Mr. F. I know I did so with my eyes open but he was so very unsettled and in such low spirits that he distractedly alluded to the river if not oil of something from the chemist's and I did it for the best.'
>
> (I, 23, 316)

What Flora is actually saying is that when Arthur acquiesced to the dissolution of their engagement, she was hysterical with grief and almost choked to death on her sobs. In referring to Mr. F.'s possible suicide she is projecting her own feelings of despair at that time onto him. She cannot say or even think that she might have considered destroying herself. Therefore she projects onto Mr. F. her own sense of desperation. On a conscious level she is unaware of her words, however, to a certain degree she knows what she is saying. Should Arthur extract from the vertiginous speech only the fact of Mr. F.'s dejection, but not her despondency, she will have succeeded in enhancing her previous desireability, showing that at the time Arthur rejected her, another suitor would have died, had she refused him. Dickens succeeds brilliantly, in revealing multiple motivations for Flora's dialogue, some consciously known to Flora, others subliminally perceived, yet all amusingly and poignantly expressed.

Another reason Flora regrets her words is that she senses an inappropriately punitive element in them. It is unseemly to be constantly reminding Arthur of his aberrant behavior. She still loves him and has to attempt to achieve her complicated objective of recapturing him by a circuitous route. When Arthur returns to England after twenty years in China, Flora immediately determines his marital status and, finding him available, proceeds simultaneously to court him and to gently reprove him. Her censure serves as an honest expression of her pain and as a strategem of her courtship. She thinks to secure him to her once again by instilling guilt in him for having rejected her. Her technique of conjuring the past has three other functions which are ancillary to her primary objective of marriage. She hopes to rectify the past by the present, to punish Arthur for his maltreatment of her, and to justify her marriage to Mr. F. She accepted Mr. F. as a compromise; since she couldn't have love she settled for comfort. Yet her unrequited love, inappropriate as it sounds coming from a middle-aged woman, has not been dispelled. The undercurrent of pain attendant upon her disappointment is ever present. Her painful past creeps into every speech and is sandwiched between her attempts to lure Arthur back and her attempts to upbraid him. She informs him that Mr. F. proposed seven times, was an excellent man, not at all like Arthur, but an excellent man. It is a reproachful, boastful and simultaneously ambiguous remark.

She is saying that adversity did not hinder Mr. F. He pursued his objective. He wanted to marry her and repeatedly proposed until he achieved his goal. His tenacity contrasts with Arthur's actions. Arthur capitulated too easily under adverse circumstances. She is also boasting that she was worthy of continued pursuit. In addition she ambiguously observes that Mr. F. was an excellent man, unlike Arthur, who was not. Simultaneously, lest that intimation be too harsh, the inference could also be that even though he was unlike Arthur, and Arthur was preferable, Mr. F. was still an admirable man.

Flora's indirect technique has two functions. It presents a double message to Arthur from which he may elect to acknowledge only that which he wants to hear, and it is a defense against her vulnerability, should Arthur reject her again, which she quickly senses he has done: " 'I know I am not what you expected, I know that very well.' " She knows she is fighting a losing battle, which is doubly painful to her. She feels she was a victim of circumstances beyond her control when their parents interfered and Arthur acquiesced in their decision. She says, " 'When your mama came and made a scene with my Papa, what was I to do?' " She is saying that it was Arthur's proper place to intervene on their behalf. Feeling victimized by parental authority and by her betrothed's capitulation to parental authority she tries to make Arthur compensate her for the victimization. Ironically, in so doing she victimizes him with her garrulity.

Appearing addle-headed, which she is not, she rivets him to the spot with her volubility. There is both a comedic and sorrowful element in the method she must devise to express a pain which surfaces in a passive and passing aggression. As a Victorian woman, she has not been conditioned to be forthright about her feelings. In fact she has been programmed to be silent about her suffering, creating a conflict between socially accepted behavior and painful feelings. Flora's conflicting emotions are unconsciously revealed by her method of expressing hostility. Her verbal technique of loquaciousness, which seems to be without focus, serves the double function of disclosing

Flora's innermost feelings and of punishing Arthur. Confronted by her kaleidoscopic delivery he becomes a captive listener.

While Arthur is in Flora's presence, he has no choice but to attend to her, as he had no alternative but to attend to the Sunday sermons of his childhood. Flora triggers thoughts of his past and when he leaves her house he reflects on his restrictive childhood, on his unloving mother and on the vanished image he once had of Mrs. Finching. Pitying "poor Flora" he relinquishes his nostalgic fantasy about her, and relegates her to the past. Flora, however, has not as yet abandoned her illusion regarding Arthur.

Three months after Arthur's call at the Casby home, Flora visits Arthur at the newly established firm of Doyce and Clennam. Surprised to see her, Arthur nonetheless welcomes her with cordiality. Flora astutely perceives his courtesy as being more civil than honest, and once again questions his sincerity. She is pained by his casual current dismissal of her and says:

> 'to go into the machinery business without so much as sending a line or card to Papa—I don't say me though there was a time but that is past and stern reality has now my gracious never mind!'
>
> (I, 23, 315)

Despite her pained remonstrances with Arthur for rejecting her a second time, Flora's intrinsic goodness comes to the fore as she explains the purpose of her visit. She has heard that Arthur is concerned for the welfare of a young person who needs additional employment and, subject to Arthur's approval, offers to give Little Dorrit a job. She knows that Amy does needlework for Arthur's mother, and while Flora is expressing her generosity, she cannot refrain from mentioning that but for his mother's touchy temper she would not have married Mr. F.

Flora divulges her basic goodness not solely by employing Little Dorrit, but also in the friendly and feminine companionship she extends to Amy. Furthermore, when Arthur is later incarcerated in the Marshalsea, Flora discloses a modesty in her compassionate effort to be of service to him without his knowledge. And at the close of the novel when she discovers that Amy and Arthur are to be married, she graciously accepts the situation. She reveals to Amy that her romantic illusions about Arthur were nonsense and adds that fate in its wisdom had decreed that a union between Arthur and herself was not ordained. She imparts the additional revelation that part of her previous desire to align herself with Arthur was due to a wish to extricate herself from the patriarchal mansion, since her father undoubtedly was " 'the most aggravating of his sex!' " Generous in defeat, she relinquishes Arthur with heartfelt good wishes for his, and for Amy's happiness.

By relegating the past to its proper perspective in history, Flora has matured to an emotional level commensurate with her chronological age. Whereas she will always retain an aspect of her fluttery manner, she will no longer be a "mermaid." In liberating herself from the past she is simultaneously freeing herself of hostility. When she relinquishes rancorous feelings, her language becomes more gentle and coherent than it had been previously. She can never entirely discard her circumlocutory speech pattern but in accepting reality she overcomes her sense of victimization and is able to extend the coherence of her phrases. She is able to string more words together with greater logic and more congruence. She does so when she begs a favor of Amy, albeit the request is made without benefit of pause. She reveals to Amy that she has been maintaining a vigil in the pie-shop across the way from the Marshalsea, during Arthur's imprisonment, in order to secretly keep him company and, at some point in the future, she would like Amy to inform him of her profound concern for his welfare, during his immurement. She says:

> 'one hope I wish to express ere yet the closing scene draws in and it is that I do trust for the sake of old times and old sincerity that Arthur will know that I didn't desert him in his misfortunes but that I came backwards and forwards constantly to ask if I could do anything for him.'
>
> (II, 34, 888)

For Flora, this is a masterpiece of lucidity, yet it retains her style. This dialogue is free from the hurt, the anger and the censure which had previously imprisoned her thoughts and muddied the focus of her words.

Continuing her conference with Amy in the same vein, Flora presents another version of clarity of thought when she says:

> 'I earnestly beg you as the dearest thing that ever was if you'll excuse the familiarity from one who moves in very different circles to let Arthur understand that I don't know after all whether it wasn't all nonsense between us though pleasant at the time.'
>
> (II, 34, 888)

This declaration is only slightly less controlled than the previous one, and in her last utterance in the novel Dickens has her revert to her customary labyrinthine form of communication lest the reader close the volume with too altered a version of his favorite character. In her final speech Flora bids adieu to Amy, returning to her former habit of circumlocution, evidently relishing her florid phrases and the effect of bewilderment they produce in Amy. Dickens is saying that Flora will never completely change and if there is some tiny spark of unconscious malice which evidences itself in her need to stun her rival Flora may be happily forgiven, for her graces outweigh her foibles.

The Cunning Function of Mr. F.'s Aunt

Dickens' most artful presentation of sublimated anger surfaces in the triad composed of Flora, Mr. F.'s Aunt and Arthur. Prior to Flora's liberation from rancor, she used Mr. F.'s Aunt as her alter ego. Cloaked in comedic form, Flora and her alter ego are not merely comic relief characters in an otherwise grim novel. They serve to carry forward the general design of a book whose structure is based on the principle of hostility. In addition to the entertainment they provide, they function as a psychological portrait of reciprocity. Each offers the other a service that neither is capable of providing for herself. Flora tenders protection; Mr. F.'s Aunt contributes animosity.

The rage Mr. F.'s Aunt shows to Arthur is a subconscious extension of the bitterness Flora feels toward him but cannot overtly express as it would appear too indecorous. Flora's acrimoniousness, stemming from the pain of having been repudiated, is vicariously eased by the Aunt's defiant ill will toward Arthur. To Flora the Aunt is a prize, someone who can give vent to hostile feeling. The Aunt's name, beginning with the noun "Mister" which is the conventional title for a male, represents a masculine ability to be aggressive without censure. Mr. F.'s Aunt is that part of Flora which might be expressed if Flora were a male, and not a female hampered by a restrictive Victorian code of behavior. Therefore Flora flaunts her relative as a valued asset. In dramatically presenting the Aunt to Arthur when she introduces her, Flora assumes a triumphant air. She is proud of the old lady and calls her "clever." She invariably compliments her for "being lively" after each of the Aunt's verbal assaults on Arthur.

Mr. F.'s Aunt, functioning in the capacity of Flora's other self, is able to provide an implicit service to Flora which the Aunt's age and eccentricity make permissible. The same remarks emanating from Flora would be considered indecent. Since it is not Flora herself, but another person, who is voicing the objectionable remarks, Flora can spare herself the self-knowledge that she is using Mr. F.'s Aunt to express her own angry feelings. Being essentially amiable, Flora can not permit herself to be as acerbic as she provides for the Aunt to be. Whereas Flora allows herself to exhibit mild hostility in pained conversations with Arthur, she revels in the fact that Mr. F.'s Aunt is so pointedly antagonistic.

At a dinner given for Arthur at the Casby home, the Aunt's first words are advanced as a general introduction to the theme of her animus toward Arthur. She immediately delivers herself of a forceful comment, one that appears to be unrelated to the occasion or to any of the assembled guests. She bellows, " 'When we lived at Henley, Barnes's gander was stole by tinkers.' " Surprisingly there is a rationale behind the hilarious non-sequitur. When we lived at Henley refers to the past (an allusion to Flora's past). Barnes's gander is analagous to Flora's gander, Arthur. A gander is the male counterpart of a goose. A goose is, in the vernacular, a fool, and the Aunt's immediate subsequent remark is that she detests a fool. The gander having been stolen by tinkers alludes to Arthur having been stolen from Flora by her father, Mr. Casby and by Arthur's mother, Mrs. Clennam, both of whom figuratively tinkered with their children's lives.

As Flora's second self, the Aunt has absorbed Arthur's maltreatment of Flora and, reflecting Flora's distress Mr. F.'s Aunt appears, throughout the novel, to be incensed by ill-usage. Consequently when she declares, " 'I hate a fool,' " she stares directly at Arthur in an attitude of extreme repugnance. On a subsequent occasion she expands on her initial acrimonius remark to Flora's former suitor by observing that " 'You can't make a head and brains out of a brass knob with nothing in it.' " The Aunt is implying that the man who jilted Flora must be a fool, and if he was a fool previously there is no hope that he will exhibit intelligence subsequently. Her observation has multileveled connotations. It verbalizes and brings into the open a rage that Flora cannot articulate; it conveys an awareness of the hopelessness of the situation which Flora can only partially accept, and it repays Flora for accepting the Aunt as a "separate legacy" which Flora is not legally obliged to do. In revealing the conflicting emotions of her loving niece, Flora's deputy functions as an echo of Flora's sublimated self and of her unspoken feelings.

In permitting Mr. F.'s Aunt to express thoughts she cannot directly voice herself, Flora is not operating out of either malice or self-knowledge, but she is deriving a vicarious thrill from the interplay which stuns and frightens Arthur, who is at a loss to understand why Mr. F's Aunt has taken so instantaneous and vehement a dislike to him. For the solicitous and charitable woman that she is, Flora displays strange hospitality in permitting the Aunt to be abusive to Arthur. Although Flora does remove the old lady from Arthur's presence on occasion, she separates them only after the Aunt has administered her customary verbal assaults to the bewildered hero.

Another instance of the Aunt's pattern of verbal mistreatment occurs when Arthur subsequently visits the Casby home on a matter of business. Sighting her target, the Aunt exclaims, " 'Drat him, if he an't come back again!' " Her vehement outcry is based on immediate cognition. She knows that he has not come for the purpose of wooing Flora, and since that is so, why is he bothering them? Why doesn't he leave them alone to accept a reality the Aunt perceives?

Flora makes no comment on the Aunt's aggressive greeting, nor does she remove her from the room, either of which course the kindly Flora might pursue if the Aunt were not her other self. Instead of remonstrating with the Aunt, she reproves Arthur, in pursuance of her fantasy of marriage. She rebukes her ex-fiancé for not having recently visited, for not having invited her out for a glass of sherry, or even a "humble sandwich." Although genuinely glad to see him, she is ambivalent about the memories his presence conjures, so she reproves him again for days gone by. This is the celebrated scene in which Flora leaves the room for a moment, cautioning Arthur in an ambiguous remark to mind the Aunt and to ignore the Aunt. She is telling him to guard Mr. F.'s Aunt, to attend to her conversation and simultaneously not to object to anything the Aunt might say. Left alone with his nemesis, Arthur is attacked by a piece of toast which the Aunt hurls at him, demanding that he eat the crust. When he disregards her command, she screams, " 'He has a proud stomach, this chap! . . . Give him a meal of chaff!' "

The Aunt's cryptic use of the term "chaff" suggests her double meaning. As a noun she is using it to signify that Arthur should be given the worthless foodstuff he deserves. As a verb it mocks him for refusing to accept her niece's offering of self, and her own offer of the crust. Since he has refused her niece, Mr. F.'s Aunt is offering him crumbs which he correctly rejects. Her mockery is not pleasant banter; it is overt enmity. When Flora returns in the midst of these hostilities, seeing Mr. F.'s

Aunt shaking her fist under Arthur's nose, she again congratulates the Aunt in an approving manner on being " 'very lively tonight.' "

Aware of the Aunt's predictable reaction to Arthur, Flora nonetheless arranges to have the irascible old lady accompany her when she visits Arthur's office on a subsequent occasion. Neither circumstance nor convention dictates Flora's action. She is prompted by an unconscious veiled aggression toward Arthur which precludes cordiality. Flora is cognizant of the vituperation that must ensue from any encounter between Arthur and Mr. F.'s Aunt, yet she enjoys the prospect of being a passive and seemingly innocent participant in the scenes the Aunt creates.

It is interesting to note the occasions on which Flora is unaccompanied by her alter ego. These are events that trigger Flora's essential goodness, which takes precedence over her need to have the Aunt act out her unresolved rancor. If Mr. F.'s Aunt were considered primarily as either chaperone or a charge for whom Flora had to provide entertainment, she would have been present in those scenes in which her absence is glaring. There are three occasions during which Flora's alternate self is absent. These events occur at the beginning, middle and end of the novel. Their significance lies in the implied meaning the Aunt's absence suggests.

An instance in which Flora's affability is in evidence but her Aunt is not occurs when Amy reports for work at the Casby household. While Little Dorrit plies her needle, Flora regales her with an account of her own history. Actually it is an appropriate setting in which Mr. F.'s Aunt could participate. Yet she is not present. If Flora were concerned solely with providing her Aunt with congenial company, what more logical opportunity than for her to join Amy and Flora in a visit? The motive for her lack of participation in this scene is that the airing of hostility is not essential to Flora's purpose. Flora is having a kindly and womanly chat with Amy.

Midway through the book, when Flora pays a visit to William Dorrit, she also does not have Mr. F.'s Aunt in tow. (Since she calls on William unescorted, the function of Mr. F.'s Aunt cannot be principally one of chaperone.) The motive for the Aunt's absence lies in the purpose of Flora's visit. Her aim is one of charity to Arthur. Rancor plays no role in her honest desire to be of help to him whenever she can. She has come to make inquiries about the villain Rigaud, seeking to rectify the stigma his disappearance has placed on the house of Clennam. It is to be an amiable visit, and Flora has no need, in Dorrit's presence, of the hostility her alter ego provides. Unacquainted with William, Flora apologizes for the intrusion, and nervous about her self-image which has been shattered by Arthur and time, inadvertently stupefies poor Dorrit by her introduction. She says:

> 'I beg Mr. Dorrit to offer a thousand apologies and indeed they would be far too few for such an intrusion which I know must be extremely bold in a lady and alone too, but I thought it would be best upon the whole however difficult though Mr. F.'s Aunt would have willingly accompanied me and as a character of great force and spirit would probably have struck one possessed of such a knowledge of life . . . '
> (II, 17, 680)

Although Flora does not, as yet, make known the purpose of her visit, which omission renders William Dorrit apoplectic, her self-introduction is enlightening to the alert reader. It suggests that despite her awareness of the impropriety of calling on William alone, she has a more important goal in reserve which is to be of service to Arthur. Her charitableness on this occasion supersedes protocol.

Flora's introduction also implies that a man with Mr. Dorrit's knowledge of life would immediately ascertain the Aunt's hostility. Even if he didn't know that the aggression was essentially directed at Clennam, the Aunt's belligerent attitude might be prejudicial to Flora's cause. Since Flora is about to enlist Dorrit's aid in helping Clennam to clear his mother's name, the likelihood that the mere mention of Arthur would elicit a derogatory comment from the Aunt and could possibly influence Dorrit against Arthur is sufficient reason to exclude the Aunt from the conference. In this scene, unlike those in which Arthur and Mr. F.'s Aunt are present, and unresolved emotions pervade Flora's feelings, there is nothing ambivalent in Flora's desire to help Arthur. She does so as a purely virtuous act. Feeling and acting out of her best instincts she has no need for the Aunt's malevolent remarks and therefore leaves her at home.

The last and most important event at which Flora's alter ego is absent occurs during the wedding ceremony of Amy and Arthur. This is the only episode in which Arthur and Flora appear in the same setting without the encumbrance of Flora's second self. The reason for the Aunt's omission from this scene is that Flora, having accepted the reality of life without Arthur, has relinquished her juvenile fantasies. No longer clinging to the past, she finds small use for the Aunt's rancorous words. Since the Aunt's primary function in the triad has been eliminated, Flora absents her from the celebration in kindly regard for the bride and groom alike—an action illustrative of Flora Casby Finching's emotional maturation.

Three Discursive Females: Mrs. Nickleby (1839), Mrs. Gamp (1844) and Mrs. Finching (1857)

The creation of Flora Casby Finching represents a significant progression in the development of Dickens' art. Psychological complexities of character and language are more subtly incorporated in his representation of Mrs. Finching than in two previous discursive females, Mrs. Nickleby and Mrs. Gamp, from whom Flora partially derives. Since these three comedic women are linked by similarities of characterization, a contrast of their portraits can be used to reveal an amplitude and profundity in *Little Dorrit* not found in the mid-career *Martin Chuzzlewit* (1844) or the early *Nicholas Nickleby* (1839).

Although Mrs. Finching does not share Mrs. Nickleby's snobbishness, some of the latter's character traits can be observed in Flora. Both women are kind; each makes repeated reference to her unjust history and alike they employ confusion as a hallmark of their speech patterns. They also share a commonality in the impact they produce on the reader and on other characters who must attend to their speech. They are alike in their capacity to evoke the discordant response of laughter and frustration. When Mrs. Nickleby is asked by Pyke and Pluck if she took cold on an outing the previous night, Mrs. Nickleby meanderingly responds:

> 'Not in the least world last night, sir . . . which is the more singular, as I am very subject to colds, indeed—very subject. I had a cold once . . . I think it was in the year eighteen hundred and seventeen; let me see, four and five are nine, and—yes, eighteen hundred and seventeen, that I thought I never should get rid of; actually and seriously, that I thought I never should get rid of. I was cured at last by a remedy that I don't know whether you ever happened to hear of, Mr. Pluck. You have a gallon of water as hot as you can possibly bear it, with a pound of salt and sixpenn'orth of the finest bran, and sit with your head in it for twenty minutes every night just before going to bed; at least, I don't mean your head—your feet. It's a most extraordinary cure—a most extraordinary cure. I used it for the first time, I recollect, the day after Christmas Day, and by the middle of April following the cold was gone.'
>
> (*NN*, 27, 421–2)

Mr. Pyke sums up the sensation of helpless frustration he undergoes at being forced to listen to Mrs. Nickleby. He indicates that "it's worth the pain of hearing" to know she recovered. Pain is the sensation Flora inflicts on Arthur when he must attend to her circumlocution, as pain is the feeling Mrs. Nickleby inflicts on Pyke when he must attend to her discursiveness.

However, there are significant differences in the characters' speech patterns. Although Mrs. Nickleby and Flora introduce distracting themes into their monologues, Mrs. Nickleby completes her sentences. Flora rarely does. Whereas Mrs. Nickleby's dialogue is circumstantial, it exhibits a stream of consciousness which allows the reader to follow how one thought reminds her of another. Flora's locution is more disjointed and more difficult to understand. She leaps in and out of topics in phrases which contain little or no punctuation and which have no grammatical construction. Through this unconventional form Dickens discloses the subject which is almost always in the forefront of Flora's mind—Arthur's rejection of her. In sequential advancement of his art, Dickens reduces grammatical guideposts for the reader who therefore has to supply the familiar constructions; he requires that the reader function in a participatory manner in order to be able to comprehend fully the poetic shorthand of the later character.

Another aspect of Dickens' developing art is his use of the externals of dress. Creating the same clothing for Mrs. Nickleby and Mrs. Gamp, Dickens expands the latter's attire to symbolize her occupation. He arrays both women in black and the two costumes assume an antithetical air of a life and death image. Mrs. Nickleby, adorning her funereal garment with juvenile ornaments wears it "with a deadly-lively air." Mrs. Gamp, wearing her black dress attends "a lying-in or a laying-out with equal zest and relish." An article of clothing which in Mrs. Nickleby represents her refusal to acknowledge her age, is developed to symbolize Mrs. Gamp's attitude toward life and death. She is equally at ease with both. She happily brings the newborn into the world and she zestfully prepares the dead for interment. The latter use of the clothing device shows a deeper and more complex portrayal of characterization.

Flora Finching evolves from a combination of some of the comedic traits found in her female predecessors, Mrs. Nickleby and Sairy Gamp. Thus Flora and Mrs. Gamp share a common fondness for alcohol; each employs an alter ego (Flora with an actual relative, Mrs. Gamp with an imaginary friend) and although the subject matter of Flora's dialogue mirrors Mrs. Nickleby's rancorous allusions to the past, Flora's disregard for syntax issues from Mrs. Gamp's phraseology. Both Flora and Sairy fracture language, and Flora's speech pattern can be observed, in fledgling form, in one of Mrs. Gamp's remarks. When Sairy informs Mr. Chuzzlewit that she and another midwife, Betsey Prig, will alternately attend to the ailing Mr.

Chuffey, Sairy expresses herself in a shorthand that will become the hallmark of Flora's style:

> 'our charges not bein' high, but wishin' they was lower and allowance made considerin' not strangers.'
>
> (MC, 46, 794)

This is the sole example of Mrs. Gamp's dialogue which displays a particular shorthand in eliminating verb and pronoun equally from her speech. But a part of her abbreviated rhetoric resurfaces in the later novel as one of the characteristic elements of Flora's style. Flora doesn't mimic Mrs. Gamp's language entirely; she merely adopts some of its grammatical forms. Flora mirrors Mrs. Gamp by occasionally omitting various pronouns from her dialogue. When she visits Arthur in the new firm of Doyce and Clennam, she says:

> 'Good gracious . . . you in the machinery and foundry way too only think, and never told us! . . . Most unkind never to have come back'

Then, curious about his partner, Flora inquires:

> 'and who can Doyce be . . . married perhaps or perhaps a daughter'

Thus Mrs. Gamp's locution appears to be the genesis of Flora's truncated sentence structure.

The evolution of characterization from Mrs. Nickleby to Mrs. Gamp to Mrs. Finching may be charted in three scenes, one from each of the novels. These three incidents reveal the increasingly complex traits, characteristics and motivations of Dickens' three characters. In each of the episodes Dickens uses an image of "choking" to divulge each woman's concern with self-image.

In *Nicholas Nickleby*, Kate Nickleby asks her mother if she has had many suitors. Mrs. Nickleby responds with a description of her lovers, which is intended to reveal her popularity when she was a young woman. She describes, in an approving manner, one suitor who emigrated. He went to Botany Bay, she says:

'in a cadet ship—a convict ship I mean—and escaped into a bush and killed sheep . . . and was going to be hung, only he accidentally choked himself, and the government pardoned him.'

In her vanity, Mrs. Nickleby displays a simplicity of mind. She has no concept of the impact of her words. She seems oblivious to the discrepancy between her usual exalted sense of class consciousness and the disrepute of the suitor she's describing. For the preservation of her self-image as a popular young woman, she includes an ex-convict among her coterie of swains.

Mrs. Nickleby shares with Mrs. Gamp a preoccupation with self-image. However, Dickens expands the latter character to disclose an absorption with the essence of self. Whereas in *Nicholas Nickleby* the "choking" incident reveals a superficial yet humorous concern with Mrs. Nickleby's injudicious taste regarding men, in *Martin Chuzzlewit* the "choking" incident with which Mrs. Gamp is involved relates to faith. Do people believe in the existence of Mrs. Harris and by extension do people have confidence in Mrs. Gamp?

For Sairy Gamp it is essential that the imaginary Mrs. Harris be validated. Mrs. Harris, who functions as Sairy's alter ego, imparts a semblance of desirable attitudes and principles to Mrs. Gamp which Mrs. Gamp does not actually possess. Without the illusion of Mrs. Harris, the image Mrs. Gamp wishes to project is destroyed. Hypocritical and toadying, Mrs. Gamp needs her second self to extend an attitude of compassion to her which she lacks. Therefore when Betsey Prig questions the existence of Mrs. Harris, Mrs. Gamp, seething with indignation, self-righteously attempts to validate her alter ego. Fighting for the essence of her projected being, she conjures not only Mrs. Harris but a whole family of Harrises to substantiate her illusory claim. She says:

'Don't I know as that dear woman is expecting of me at this minnit, . . . and is a-lookin' out of window down the street, with little Tommy Harris in her arms . . . his own I have been, ever since I found him . . . with his small red worsted shoe a-gurglin' in his throat, where he had put it in his play, a chick, wile they was leavin' of him on the floor a-lookin' for it through the ouse and him a-choakin' sweetly in the parlour!'

(*MC*, 49, 837)

In Mrs. Gamp's attempt to corroborate the existence of Mrs. Harris, by manufacturing Tommy Harris imagistically suffocating, Sairy is, like Mrs. Nickleby, unconscious of her words. "Choakin' sweetly" is a bizarre description of someone in the throes of choking to death. The adverb substantiates Mrs. Gamp's unusual attraction to death.

Whereas vain Mrs. Nickleby is not rendered simplistically, by comparison with Mrs. Gamp her portrait may be considered superficial. Mrs. Gamp's more complicated personality offers evidence of Dickens' continuing artistic advancement. Sairy and her imaginary alter ego, Mrs. Harris, are the forerunners of Dickens' subtle portrait of Flora and her alter ego, Mr. F.'s Aunt.

In *Little Dorrit* the "choking" incident occurs in the scene in which Flora pays a visit to Doyce and Clennam and Arthur evinces a surface cordiality. "Though not altogether enraptured" at the sight of Mr. F.'s Aunt and her niece, he is polite. Flora perceives that he is far from gratified at her visit, and rebukes him for the insincerity of his greeting. Launching into the past she is, unlike her predecessors, aware of what she is saying. She is aware of having confused her metaphors, and she is also cognizant of the effect her confusion and complaint have on Arthur. In a perceptive evaluation of the impact she has on him, she says:

'but I dare say you know what I mean and if you don't you don't lose much and care just as little I will venture to add—when they severed the golden bond that bound us and threw us into fits of crying on the sofa nearly choked at least myself.'

(I, 23, 316)

Condensing time and events, Flora's speech is doubly reproachful of Arthur. It indicates that she was more adversely affected than he by their youthful separation. Furthermore, it signifies that she is aggrieved by his current disinterest, which she finds equally insupportable.

Flora's tearful "choking" incorporates nuances of character not discernible in the more obvious vignettes of Sairy and Mrs. Nickleby. Flora's reproachful disposition to Arthur is similar to Mrs. Nickleby's reproving attitude toward her late husband. Flora's hysterical choking also issues from, and is an extension of Mrs. Gamp's need for the imaginary Tommy Harris, whose existence authenticates the image Sairy wants to project. Flora needs Arthur to validate her actuality by evincing interest in her. Implicit in his disinterestedness is the fact that he has rescinded past connections and erased her from consciousness. For him she no longer exists.

Flora's self-image is shattered by Arthur's lack of attention. Her concern differs from Mrs. Gamp's fantastical public posturings. For Mrs. Finching the problem is not one of Arthur's belief in her public image; it is a matter of Clennam's acknowledgement of her essence, even if his neighborliness is unalloyed by romance. Flora rebukes him as much for his dismissal of her as a human being as for his rejection of her as a lover. Sincere regard and attention to her as a person would be an appropriate manifestation of his remorse, and her reproofs center on that theme. He doesn't remember her, denies her presence and therefore implicitly disavows her existence. Dickens' characterization of Flora is a more subtle and complex rendering of self and the psychological requirements of selfhood than the portraits of either Mrs. Nickleby, or Mrs. Gamp, from whom Mrs. Finching is partially derived.

Progressively expanding on the creation of Mrs. Nickleby who is supported financially by her children, into the picture of Mrs. Gamp who is assisted in her morality by the illusory Mrs. Harris, Dickens fashions Flora, who is emotionally financed by her alter ego in subtle reciprocity. However, Dickens adds a redemptive dimension to Flora's psychological development. Unlike her comical predecessor, Mrs. Gamp, who has no morally redeeming features and must therefore continue to look to a projected image of self through the eyes of Mrs.

Harris, Flora is able to relinquish her second self in favor of a sustaining individuality. She eventually liberates herself from the behavioral support the Aunt supplies and from the identity she had vainly hoped to acquire from Arthur. She can ultimately support herself psychically on the strength of her own moral fiber. In creating Flora with her initial need for a surrogate, and developing her so that she becomes a character who can ultimately stand alone, Dickens leads Flora away from a route of dependence to one of independence, testifying to the growing profundity and complexity of his maturing artistic imagination.

4

Interaction: Misleading Surface Images

Amy and Fanny: Sibling Rivalry

In his customary deceptive style, in evidence throughout *Little Dorrit*, Dickens presents an anatomy of the love, hate and competition that animates the interactions between the Dorrit sisters. Hidden facets of their rivalrous dependencies surface upon close examination of their relationship. Dickens' artful aim is to betray the surface images he has created of Amy's virtue and Fanny's wickedness.

The notion that Amy's love for Fanny is not reciprocated is a false one into which the reader is beguiled due to Fanny's wrath. Her ire, however, is frequently followed by expressions of remorse, and her regret contains elements of love for Little Dorrit. When, as heirs to a large fortune, the Dorrit family is about to drive away from the prison, it is Fanny, not Dorrit, who notices and comments on Amy's absence. Immediately afterward, Fanny spies Little Dorrit being carried out of the Marshalsea in her shabby black dress. Enraged, Fanny decries her sister's attire as infamous and disgraceful, calling it "romantic nonsense of the lowest kind" for Amy to continue to wear threadbare garments. When Arthur tells the Dorrits that Amy has fainted, Fanny bursts into tears and says:

'Dear Amy, open your eyes, that's a love! Oh Amy, Amy, I really am so vexed and ashamed. Do rouse yourself, darling.'

(I, 36, 481)

Fanny shows a concern for Little Dorrit not exhibited by any other member of the family, although all are present in the carriage. Fanny's regard for her sister supersedes her anger with Amy for obstinately refusing to alter her mode of dress despite the fact that Fanny has repeatedly begged her to do so. Dickens establishes this pattern of wrath followed by remorse to indicate Fanny's feelings of tenderness toward her sister and her desire to make reparations.

A pattern of indignation and atonement emerges in the interplay between the two young women. Fanny's resentment is overt; Amy's is covert. In an effort to make restitution during her remorseful periods, Fanny displays physical proofs of her affection. She hugs, kisses and reaches out to Amy in demonstrations of contrition for the abuse she inflicts on Little Dorrit. Demonstrativeness flows only from Fanny toward Amy. Amy does not physically approach Fanny. Her lack of physical response to Fanny cannot be attributed to a dislike of physical contact since she is excessively demonstrative to her father. Amy's restraint in touching Fanny can be attributed to a justifiable resentment of Fanny's abusive behavior and part of the artful way in which she manages to project an image of martyrdom, which carries its own feature of vexation for Fanny.

Amy incites Fanny's irritability by pretending to innocence and virtue. These poses are indirect ways of presenting herself as superior to Fanny. Amy's subtle competitive behavior is disclosed on the Grand Canal when the sisters are conversing in a gondola, hesitantly pursued by Sparkler. The conversation turns on Sparkler's mother. Fanny accurately declares that Mrs. Merdle is "as insolent and false as any woman in the world" and that since the Dorrits have inherited wealth, Mrs. Merdle treats Fanny with respect. Nonetheless, Fanny is still smarting from Mrs. Merdle's previous scorn. She is enraged, not only with Mrs. Merdle, but with herself for the fact that cupidity and circumstance impelled her to accept a bribe of a bracelet on condition that she stop seeing Sparkler. Fanny correctly intuits that Mrs. Merdle's deception in pretending to have met Fanny

abroad for the first time is intended to obliterate the embarrassing incident of the bracelet. Amy wants to know why Mrs.
Merdle would enact such a pretense. Fanny responds with
annoyance:

> 'Why? Good gracious, my love!' (again very much in the tone of You
> stupid little creature) 'how can you ask? Don't you see that I may have
> become a rather desirable match for a noodle? And . . . of considering
> our feelings?'
>
> (II, 6, 551)

Part of the reason for Fanny's vexation is that implicit in Amy's
question is the idea that Amy wouldn't stoop to deceit, and
Fanny knows this to be a false image Amy is attempting to
project. Amy's effort to pretend that she would honor the
abstract ideal of truth under all circumstances is a distortion of
the reality by which she herself lives.

Amy's pretense of virtue is, in part, a subtle form of
competition with her sister, since she's using innocence to
indicate a superiority to Fanny. The nature of her question is
intended to reflect honor upon herself. It is supposed to signify
the purity that innocence connotes. But her query is, by
implication, a trap. If Fanny knows the answer, which she
does, her knowledge suggests a worldliness qualitatively less
compatible with goodness than Amy's innocence. Amy has
therefore scored a victory in the battle for supremacy.

With a single question Amy is able to provide herself with a
double opportunity to triumph over her sister. She knows from
experience that any declaration or interrogation purporting to
reveal her immaculacy is going to vex Fanny. By irritating her
sister, Amy paradoxically places herself in a position from
which she may then exhibit another form of pseudo-piety, by
meekly accepting Fanny's ire.

Although Amy's provocative question discloses a subtle
form of hostility, her humility imparts an image of virtue to her
character, which temporarily minimizes her low self-esteem.
Her submissiveness stems from a misperceived sense of worth-
lessness, due to, and fostered by, her family's contempt for her

prison birth, and hence for her. Fanny does not let Amy forget her birth in the Marshalsea, and makes repeated demeaning references to it. Whether her slurs take the form of vituperative reminders: " 'you complete prison-child' " or casual reminders: " 'I was not born where you were, you know, Amy, and perhaps that makes a difference,' " Fanny frequently stigmatizes her sister for her prison birth. Fanny's diminution of Amy reinforces the latter's low self-esteem which perpetuates her sense of unworthiness. Simultaneous with her low self-image is a resentment of the inferior status to which the family assigns her. Her indignation manifests itself obliquely. She is too timid to express her displeasure directly, and engages in subtle slurs to imply that Fanny is less virtuous than she. Since Fanny stigmatizes her for having been born in prison, Amy has a need to appear respectable to her sister. If she did not feel inferior she would have no need to compete for the honor of being the more admirable of the sisters. Her false humility is an indirect effort to achieve respectability, but it functions paradoxically as an irritant to Fanny. Amy's desire to be valued, like Fanny's, is one that stems from the humiliation of her heritage. Unlike Fanny, who overtly declares her hatred of the Marshalsea and of the past, Amy copes with her sense of dishonor in her customary manner of denial. She disavows her degradation by enunciating her love of prison and her life there. In order to prove that she is unashamed of her roots, Amy repudiates her fortunate present condition as well as her ignominious history. Her unacknowledged shame, in turn, serves to exacerbate her timidity.

Although normally too meek to assert herself, at one juncture in their wealthy state, Amy does offer a reproach to Fanny when the latter denounces her for having befriended Pet Meagles Gowan. Pet is a revered friend of Arthur Clennam, who knows the Dorrits' background. Mr. Dorrit, his son Tip, and his daughter Fanny want desperately to excise memories of their poverty and Fanny castigates Amy for aiding Pet since Pet is a friend of Arthur's and Arthur is a reminder of their painful past. In a rare rebuke to Fanny's censure, Amy says, " 'I never offend you wilfully Fanny . . . though you are so hard with me!' "

Amy's retort to her sister is a partial denial of intent. Part of the statement is, however, true. Amy does not consciously want to offend Fanny. She does so subconsciously. Amy's reproach is more an effort to instill guilt in Fanny than it is an assertion of her right to befriend whomever she wants. Little Dorrit's method of attempting to induce a sense of culpability in Fanny is an integral part of the sisters' continuing struggle for supremacy. It is a competition in which Fanny eagerly joins. However, she does not succumb to the provocative ploy; instead she lectures Amy on responsible behavior. She declares that if Amy humiliates her accidentally, then she ought to be more careful of her conduct.

Complex and compelling motivations generally trigger Amy's "accidental" manner of embarrassing and thus enraging Fanny. In the aforementioned scene, none of the contributing forces focuses primarily on Amy's right, as a human being, to aid Pet Gowan in her unhappy marriage. One reason that Amy seeks an acquaintance with Pet is that she has promised Arthur to do so. In this regard she is functioning as Arthur's delegate. Another motive is fed by her inquisitiveness; Little Dorrit has a curiosity to know more about the young woman in whom Arthur displays so strong an interest. An additional and subliminal reason for befriending Pet relates to Amy's justifiable resentment at Fanny. Assisting Pet is a subtle and innocuous way in which an apparently virtuous act will result (as Amy knows from experience) in goading her sister. Too meek to engage in direct confrontation with Fanny, Amy wounds her in these subtle ways. She engages in actions which have, as part of their motive, a method of retaliation for the pain inflicted on her by Fanny. Amy chooses, as her battlefield, Fanny's area of extreme sensitivity: her desire for respectability. Fanny's greatest vulnerability lies in her sense of shame regarding the family's prison heritage, a sense that needs continual proofs and emblems of esteem to counteract it. Therefore any action that Fanny might construe or misconstrue as offending the family dignity, becomes a successful arena in which Amy can retaliate.

This pattern of interplay between Fanny and Amy stems from a competition whose function it is to determine who is the more virtuous or superior in any given situation. Fanny overtly flaunts her greater knowledge of high society and Amy covertly parades her moral excellence. Neither girl is true to herself. Fanny denies the past in too great a regard for status, and Amy eschews the present in too high an estimate of former times. Neither can incorporate the past, in its rightful sphere, into the present. In their current situation, Fanny's riches have brought her a partial image of respectability and an opportunity to achieve the social mobility toward which she is continually striving. Amy's efforts to undermine the image Fanny wishes to preserve are a perpetual source of Fanny's rage at her sister, which is the reason Fanny remarks that even so insolent a woman as Sparkler's mother pretends to have forgotten that she once bribed Fanny with a bracelet. Fanny stresses Mrs. Merdle's current civility to the Dorrits as a reminder to Amy that social deceptions are partially enacted to spare another's feelings. But Amy sees nothing wrong in acknowledging the humiliating occasion on which Fanny and Mrs. Merdle initially met. Amy says, " 'We can always go back to the plain truth.' "

Amy's apparent concern with veracity is misleading. It is not habitual adherence to truth that is paramount in her mind, but that their previous life should not be forgotten. Her unwillingness to surrender old times is an overriding subject of discord between the sisters. Amy's earlier reluctance to change her shabby black dress for more suitable attire when Mr. Dorrit was released from prison is symbolic of her general inability to adapt to new circumstances and new ways of being. Her disinclination to discard her prison garments is also symptomatic of her refusal to relinquish a previous stage of her life in order to enjoy her current affluent status. Amy's obsession with her early and recent history is a source of anguish to her sister, which is not motivated solely by Fanny's snobbery. Amy stirs Fanny's feelings of humiliation by her obsessive reminders

of a wretched past. If Fanny were able to persuade her sister to
forgo the constant reminders, her own sense of disgrace would
diminish. Fanny's outraged pretentiousness functions as cam-
ouflage for her sense of shame, and her rage is an expression of
that odious condition. Despite her affectations, Fanny makes a
pertinent and poignant plea to Amy when she cries, " 'Are we
never to be permitted to forget?' "

Fanny is not the sole member of the Dorrit clan to be
adversely affected by Amy's references to their former life. Her
reminders are likewise a source of pain to her father and her
brother. Tip has made a mild request of Amy to refrain from
addressing him by his prison name. He prefers his Christian
name of Edward, but Amy repeatedly forgets and calls him Tip.
Dorrit corroborates his other childrens' distress when he refers
to the agony of their incarceration. He complains to Amy,
" 'You alone, and only you—constantly revive the topic.' "
Amy imprisons herself and the family alike by her memorials to
a time gone by.

The past and present differ in one aspect of the sisters'
relationship. In former years Amy pursued Fanny. During the
period of their altered fortunes it is Fanny who seeks Amy's
company. However, there's a difference in the sisters' motivations. When Amy sought out Fanny at the theater where the
latter worked, Amy's purpose was not one of camaraderie but
rather of meddlesomeness, which Fanny surmised with her
customary acuity. She said," 'Well! And what have you got on
your mind, Amy? Of course you have got something on your
mind about me!' " Amy was anxious to know the particulars
concerning the bracelet Mrs. Merdle had given Fanny. Amy's
interest had, as its primary source, her need to be aware of
everything that went on in the family, so as not to relinquish
control of her matriarchal position.

During the period of their altered fortune Fanny reaches out
to Amy, not to oversee her activities, nor to use her as a
drudge, but to share a sisterly camaraderie with her, to share
her thoughts, feelings and dilemmas. Fanny's most significant
problem is Sparkler. She perceives him to be " 'an idiot in a

state of desperation . . . dying for a glimpse of [her].' " She shares this perception with Amy and adds that Sparkler is only " 'waiting to get his courage up' " to call on her. Amy's response is to inquire, " 'Will you see him?' " On the surface Amy's question is innocuous, but it contains a judgmental feature. The critical nuance is predicated on Fanny's response. Should Fanny's answer be in the affirmative, she stands the chance of Amy offering a mild reproof. Amy's reproach would focus on Fanny's lack of integrity in encouraging a man she considers a "noodle."

Fanny doesn't become irate at the question. Instead she gives Amy the benefit of the doubt as to her motive in asking, and inquires what she means by the question. Amy's response is equivocal. She says, " 'I mean . . . I think I rather mean what do you mean, dear Fanny?' " The reason Amy equivocates is that she fears Fanny's wrath, and the justification for her trepidation is that subconsciously she knows that her apparently innocuous question is a trap for Fanny to show her lack of integrity, at which point Amy would have scored another victory in their battle for supremacy. Amy would have been the victor of virtuous behavior by comparison with Fanny's lack of it.

Fanny had previously indicated, in one of their many skirmishes, that it was not Amy's place continually to be forgiving Fanny and placing Fanny in the untenable position of being morally instructed by her younger sister. In the foregoing exchange, which does not become a skirmish because Amy retreats verbally, it is similarly not appropriate for Amy to judge Fanny. Yet it is part of the pattern of her interaction with her sister to be censorious, which usually precipitates Fanny's rage. Both girls are in the habit of judging one another deprecatingly; Fanny does it overtly; Amy covertly.

Despite their continuing warfare they offer one another companionship. Though Amy's pseudo-purity is irritating to Fanny, she continues to reach out to Amy and Amy is always available to her. Though Fanny's volatile friendship is offered in part as a charity, Amy gratefully accepts it because it provides fellowship and saves her from total isolation.

The degree of Amy's solitude has increased with the family's wealth. Money and position have combined to increase Amy's marginality within the family structure. She is no longer needed by Mr. Dorrit, therefore her closeness and service to her father are curtailed, and her status as family drudge is jeopardized. She feels diminished, and with the exception of her expanded association with Fanny, she cannot enjoy her new position in society. Nor can she enjoy the pleasures of travel. The beauties of Italy are lost to her. The shadows on Venetian waters serve only to remind her that she is more marginal at the time of her heightened success than during the period she struggled to achieve the glory from which she is now almost totally alienated. She cannot respond to Venetian architecture or nature without a nostalgic yearning to return to the Marshalsea, where within its familiar confines she was able to maintain the position of being needed by the family. The psychological scars of a prison birth are not eradicated by wealth. Success has made her a supernumerary, at least in her relationship with her father. Therefore the connection with Fanny, albeit far from ideal, is of special importance to Amy.

At a subsequent conference between the sisters, Fanny confides her wavering ambition to marry Sparkler. Amy expresses horror at the thought and says, " 'I would far rather we worked for a scanty living again, than I would see you rich and married to Mr. Sparkler.' " Invoking the past again, Amy fears the future since she has a personal stake in Fanny's betrothal. Aside from the fact that Amy thinks Fanny is worthy of a more intelligent mate than Sparkler, there is another motive for her demurral; if Fanny marries, Amy would lose the close association that has been built up between them. Since their acquisition of wealth Amy has become distanced from her father. She has been symbolically and geographically separated from him and the vacuum left by William has been partially filled by Fanny. With Fanny's marriage an actual separation of the sisters would occur and Amy would be doubly bereft.

She has been deprived of the closeness she once had with her father. The functions she used to perform and which gave her a sense of purpose and power, are no longer commensurate with the conventions of the society in which the Dorrits move. Heretofore she acted as a loyal and loving helpmeet to Mr. Dorrit, and as overseer of the family. She worked, cooked, cleaned, and mended for her father. In constant attendance on him, she provided comfort and housewifely solicitude. With riches and respectability, all her loving chores are lost to her. Now a coterie of servants perform her duties. She resides in a palatial room far removed from her father's quarters, and sees him but infrequently. Fanny is Amy's one continuing link with family, her connection with social life. When Fanny is off on her rounds of society activities, Amy is alone on her balcony, dreaming of the Marshalsea and of the significance of her position in the family in the days gone by. In Amy's comparatively meaningless current existence Fanny is her one strong bond to the past, and she dreads to lose that tie.

Dread of loss is the reason Amy behaves in an unusual way when Fanny tells her of her engagement to Sparkler. She initiates a spontaneous embrace of Fanny. She falls on her bosom and cries there. This demonstrative show of affection is the first and only time Amy physically reaches out to Fanny, and Fanny responds to the embrace. She lays her cheek against Amy's and they cry together. Amy cries for the loss of continuity; Fanny cries for the loss of integrity. The mutuality of their embrace momentarily unites them in pain and love. Both girls cry for a lack that the marriage will bring; Amy for a want of closeness; Fanny for an absence of love.

Fanny is not going into the marriage with romantic notions. She is marrying for status and revenge. She is self-aware regarding her character and her motives. When Amy cautions her against a life of revenge, Fanny states that such a life is the one to which she is best suited. " 'I am better fitted for such a life than for almost any other.' " When Amy raises an objection to the amount of time Fanny has known Sparkler, Fanny indicates that the length of time is not a factor in her decision.

She is impatient to combine social mobility with revenge. She is socially and psychologically impatient. Dickens explains the forces that have produced her and that motivate her actions when he has her say to Amy:

> 'Other girls, differently reared and differently circumstanced altogether might wonder at what I say or may do. Let them. They are driven by their lives and characters; I am driven by mine.'
>
> (II, 14, 649)

In his desire to show the social and psychological forces that shape both girls' characters and motivate their behavior, Dickens presents a deceptive portrait of the interaction between the Dorrit sisters. What surfaces as Fanny's hostility toward Amy is, in reality, one manifestation of her ambivalent feelings toward her younger sister. Amy's apparent concern for Fanny is actually one manifestation of her ambivalence toward her older sister. On the surface theirs appears to be an unfair relationship, with Amy giving all and Fanny taking all, but on a deeper level Dickens is revealing a complicated interplay of reciprocity by which both young women benefit and in which they equally compete for power. In their competition for supremacy Amy's false humility conflicts with Fanny's quest for respectability and sets the pattern for their hostile interaction. Their unseemly interplay is complicated by a love and dependence which draws them close in the era of their altered circumstances. Their love and dependence is reciprocal. Fanny depends on Amy as an outlet for her wrath and as a vehicle into which she can pour out her heart. Amy relies on Fanny as a replacement for her father and as someone who needs her within the family structure. Additionally both girls retain a sense of their marginality within the societal structure, which has an effect of binding them closer together, although it is simultaneously an area of great discord between them. Their sense of marginality stems from too onerous a past, to which neither can allocate an appropriate place in the present.

Dickens examines their current lives in terms of their past. His anatomy of the love, hate and competition that exist between the sisters is a painstaking analysis of the social and psychological forces which are manifest in the girls' interactions and which produce their interactions. Dickens' deceptive prose style paradoxically reveals as it conceals the hidden forces that operate beneath the surface of their interplay. He shows their reciprocal need for one another and the pain each inflicts on the other. His profound characterization of Fanny and Amy mitigates the initial impression he creates on the surface, of snob and saint. He uses the device of a bracelet as a vehicle through which to demonstrate the various motives underlying the behavior of both women. The bracelet functions as a focal point of Fanny's revenge at Mrs. Merdle, as a focus of Amy's judgmental attitude toward Fanny, and as a means of divulging Amy's intrusiveness.

Arthur and Mrs. Clennam: Reaching Out

In another deceptive relationship calculated to evoke quick surface recognition of dramatis personae, Dickens presents a misleading portrait of the interaction between vindictive Mrs. Clennam and her self-deprecating son Arthur. The underlying motif in the interplay of the hero and his mother is one of the need for, and the fear of, tenderness. Ostensibly the emotional requirements of mother and son are antithetical. Arthur yearns for affection; Mrs. Clennam spurns it. However, Dickens suggests that beneath the surface both characters require, dread and reject compassion when it is offered. Mother and son are ambivalent about the gentler emotions.

Mrs. Clennam's aloofness is a manifestation of her fear of intimacy. She correctly equates tenderness with love and flees from it. Arthur's remoteness is a manifestation of his unfamiliarity with warmheartedness. He perceives himself unworthy of it and is therefore blind to its presence. Mother and son's symbolic flight from love results in their cold and unfeeling interaction.

Mrs. Clennam's disquietude with tenderness stems from her own religious training. Reared under the philosophy of Calvinism, her terror of love is a reaction to, and a deference to, a repressive and punitive faith. Hiding her fear of affection under a glacial exterior, Mrs. Clennam frequently reacts to Arthur with detachment. When Arthur returns home after twenty years, Mrs. Clennam responds according to her custom: she gives him "one glassy kiss, and four stiff fingers muffled in worsted."

Although Mrs. Clennam's religious philosophy induces and gives sanction to her undemonstrative behavior, she hesitantly attempts to reach out to her son. Her tentative and fleeting efforts at tenderness are obscured by her stoniness and by her physical condition. Underneath her cold exterior Mrs. Clennam is in physical pain. Paralyzed for many years, she attributes her paralysis to rheumatism or "nervous weakness." In part she is correct: she has a nervous weakness. It is her vulnerability to pain. She expresses her pain in an ambiguous, distancing and poignant remark when she prepares to retire for the evening. She says, " 'Good-night, Arthur. Affery will see to your accommodation. Only touch me, for my hand is tender.' "

Her last sentence is a relenting, affecting and ambiguous remark. It is less severe than her previous cold comment that the housekeeper will see to Arthur's comfort. It is a poignant comment in that it denotes pain, both physical and psychic. Furthermore, it is moving in its ambiguity. It could mean: "Don't touch me. I cannot bear to be touched. Touching causes too much suffering and I am already in pain." Or it could also mean: "Only touch me. Do touch me. Let me feel your closeness." She is, in fact, saying that even though she is in physical distress she still wants to feel Arthur's touch. Underneath her glacial exterior is a distorted effort at rapprochement. If her feelings were not confused she would tell him unequivocally not to touch her, which would eliminate the possibility of any contact. If it were her sole intent to prevent contact, she would not offer an explanation for her forewarning. Her explanation signifies that she feels it necessary to justify her cautionary comment lest it appear too harsh. Her reason for validating the remark is a further attempt to relent after the coldness of her preceding sentence. Although she prevents him, physically and symbolically, from coming too close, she does not stop him completely from coming into physical contact with her.

The idea of physicality is painful to Mrs. Clennam on a psychological level. If there were no subconscious feeling in her for her son she would say nothing. Her aloof demeanor would invite his reserved or cursory response. If she were only in physical pain she would not permit him to touch her at all lest his touch exacerbate the pain. She wants to be touched and she fears being touched. She wants to reach out to Arthur yet dreads rejection.

Her fear of rejection has as its basis the knowledge that Arthur has never loved her as she "once half-hoped he might." In addition, she knows that his return to England, after his father's demise, has not been primarily due to his desire to see her. She has been hurt by his long delay in returning to England and tells him so in her customarily frigid manner, which glosses over her pain. On the day after his return Arthur asks his mother if she is inclined to discuss business. She replies:

> 'Am I inclined, Arthur? Rather, are you? Your father has been dead for a year and more. I have been at your disposal, and waiting your pleasure, ever since.'
>
> (I, 5, 84)

She is saying that she would have wanted him to evince an interest in her before such a long time had elapsed. In a way she is saying the same thing to him that Flora said. She is saying: "Notice me."

Arthur is impervious to her pain and hears only her displeasure. Replying to the latter element in her dialogue he indicates that his delay in returning was the result of his desire to give her time to transact the necessary business arrangements attendant upon the House of Clennam. He does not indicate any desire to see her after having been away for twenty years.

Arthur fails to indicate a wish to see Mrs. Clennam because

he is ambivalent about being in her presence. Although he is a "grave dark man of forty," Arthur still reacts to his mother as though he were a small, cowed child, overwhelmed by the physical superiority and authority of Mrs. Clennam. He doesn't view her as an invalid, isolated from the world by her self-imposed imprisonment. He doesn't regard himself as Mrs. Clennam's only familial link. He perceives her as an unloving punitive parent and himself as a resentful child-man. He is oblivious to the need underlying her wish for a partnership. He doesn't notice that she wants to maintain a continuing relationship with him. He is aware solely of her possible anger should he refuse to go into partnership with her. Actually he is correct and she does display anger. During their discussion she anticipates his decision to abandon the House of Clennam and registers "bitter disappointment."

Arthur abandons her on two levels; he will not go into business with her and he will not reside in the same dwelling with her. Both refusals relate to the house which symbolizes Mrs. Clennam's essence. It is a funereal residence, airless and grim. No light penetrates its dark interior. The house is a symbol of the interior of Mrs. Clennam's soul. It is the spirit of lovelessness which has been the hallmark of Mrs. Clennam's life. With the return of her son she experiences a glimmer of hope for a partial alteration of her situation. She not only expects that Arthur will carry on the family business, but she anticipates that he will reside in the house with her. If she had not expected him to stay she would have asked what his plans were for lodging, but she does not. She assumes that he will live with her and therefore merely mentions that Affery will attend to his needs.

The house is also Mrs. Clennam's connection with life, albeit a distorted, confining and destructive link. Yet Arthur advises her to abandon the house. He speaks of it as an anomaly and an anachronism. He reminds her that it is failing as a business venture. He tells her that whereas she had been an active woman she has grown old and cannot keep pace with the times. She listens to his enumeration of her failing powers and says:

> 'Do you consider . . . that a house serves no purpose, Arthur, in sheltering your infirm and afflicted . . . mother?'

(I, 5, 85)

She is appealing to him on a personal level. Revealing psychic pain, she is trying to elicit a modicum of sympathy from Arthur. She is asking him, in the only way she knows, to have compassion for her age and infirmity. She does not refer to herself in the first person. She refers to herself as his mother (which she is not) since that is what she wants to be and it is as his mother that she is entreating him.

Arthur does not know that Mrs. Clennam is not his natural mother. She has kept his background a secret. Arthur is the son of Mr. Clennam and a young singer. When Mrs. Clennam discovered that her husband loved another woman and had had a child by her, she vengefully forced Arthur's mother to give him up to her and to renounce all claim to the child. She has guarded her secret and reared Arthur as her own. Although she had reared him punitively and strictly according to her Calvinist doctrine, she has viewed him as her own. She is speaking to him as though he were her biological offspring. In referring to herself as his mother she is attempting to reach Arthur on a human and familial plane.

Arthur's response denies her supplication and invalidates her appeal. He says, " 'I was speaking only of business purposes.' " Arthur is impervious to her request. An alienated, introverted and unappealing hero, he is blind to other people's needs. He takes no notice of Mrs. Clennam. He gives no recognition to her disguised entreaty.

Arthur's insensitivity to his mother follows a pattern similar to those established by his relations with other women characters in the novel. As he takes no notice of Mrs. Clennam's entreaty, so does he ignore Flora except when he needs her to supply him with information. Early on in the novel, he pays heed to Amy for the purpose of extracting certain facts from her. Later on, when Little Dorrit's inclination toward him takes a romantic turn, he declines for an inordinately long time, to give credence to her womanliness. His reaction to Affery, the old, faithful and attentive housekeeper, is similarly unfeeling. He does not accord her the singular pleasure of nurturing him with food and drink. His interactions with these women are primarily based on his perception of their usefulness to him relative to his business interests. All of these four women offer him love in their own fashion but he is blind to love whenever it is extended. On a symbolic level he is responding to them as though he were offering them "one glassy kiss and four stiff fingers."

Arthur's cold but civil treatment of his mother is motivated by his bitter resentment of her strict and stern rearing. He is meting out retribution to her as she measured out punishment to his father and to him. Although Arthur supposes himself to be her son (he has no reason not to) his response is a cold denial of filial feeling. He is placing the relationship on a strictly business plane, and he will soon inform his mother that he does not want any part of the Clennam House even on a business basis. He will indicate shortly that he plans to abandon his participation in the firm altogether.

Arthur's rejection of the family enterprise is not due solely to his concern about the honesty of the firm's negotiations. If he were primarily interested in rectifying what he accurately suspects to be dishonest transactions, what better way to redress wrongs than for him to assume his rightful place as Mrs. Clennam's partner and to set about making reparations to any injured party? His refusal to participate in the establishment's affairs has, as one of its motives, a need to wound his mother. His disengagement is not motivated by a desire to pursue another occupation. He has no urgent wish to express himself in another field of endeavor. His primary impulse is to exercise opposition to Mrs. Clennam. Yet in so doing he wants for her to show a kind regard for him. As she wishes for, but does not receive, a tender response from him, so he requires, but does not know how to elicit, a gentle rejoinder from her.

Cowed by her as though he were still a boy, he unsuccessfully attempts to draw forth appreciation for past obediences. In a negatively worded plea, he says:

> 'I cannot say that I believe my forty years have been profitable or pleasant to myself, or anyone; but I have habitually submitted, and I only ask you to remember it.'
>
> (I, 5, 86)

He is telling her that under his parents' aegis he has been miserable, wounding her again. Mrs. Clennam immediately erects her icy barrier and in turn gives no heed to her son's entreaty. She responds coldly: " 'Have you finished, Arthur, or have you anything more to say to me? I think there can be nothing else.' "

The balance of power has shifted as Arthur becomes the suppliant and Mrs. Clennam the unyielding force. It switches again, however, as Arthur pursues a matter that has recently been of constant concern to him. He has perceptively entertained a suspicion relevant to the ethics of the family business. His uncertainty regarding the firm's morality has been haunting him since his father's death, at which time the elder Clennam's dying motions seemed to Arthur to signal a deep remorse. From his father's feeble utterance, "your mother," and his anxious fingering of his watch, Arthur deduced that the timepiece was to be mailed to Mrs. Clennam. Carrying out his trust, and spying the watch on her desk during his first visit home, Arthur leans close to his mother and whispers:

> 'Is it possible, mother that [father] had unhappily wronged any one, and made no reparation?
> . . . .
> For Heaven's sake, let us examine sacredly whether there is any wrong entrusted to us to set right.'
>
> (I, 5, 87–8)

Mrs. Clennam's first reaction is to physically distance herself from her son. She abruptly sits back in her wheelchair and stares at him in fixed, angry silence. Undaunted by her wrathful glare, Arthur presses the accusation further. He indicates that he not only suspects his father of having grievously injured someone financially, but charges his mother with having been the moving force behind the unlawful deed.

Mrs. Clennam's immediate reaction demonstrates the intensity of the pain her son has caused. She throws an arm up "as if he were striking at her, and she warding off the blow." In the succeeding moments her pain gives way to heightened anger which mounts to a murderous rage. Misusing spiritual commentary, she tells Arthur that in previous times pious men would have cursed their sons for less of an outrage than he has committed against her by his accusation, that pious men would have sent their sons forth to be ostracized and to perish. She wrathfully threatens to renounce him if he should ever accuse her again.

Mrs. Clennam's terror-stricken fury is based on the veracity of her son's allegations. She has altered the codicil to a will which would have left a legacy to Frederick Dorrit, and upon his death to his niece, Amy. She has withheld a legacy rightfully belonging to the Dorrits, the funds of which would have enabled William to pay the debt for which he has been incarcerated for a quarter of a century. She has engaged in this immoral and criminal act out of her need for revenge against the Dorrits, since Frederick had once befriended the young singer who was Arthur's mother.

Mrs. Clennam, using a distorted version of religion to sanction her nefarious dealings, has taken it upon herself to be God's emissary in punishing the Dorrits. On a religious level she believes her behavior to be justified. Subconsciously, however, she knows her deportment to have been unwarranted and therefore metes out punishment to herself in the form of paralysis. Her physical impairment is a physiological manifestation of guilt for reprehensible conduct, which in turn, creates her self-imposed imprisonment.

She rationalizes her censurable action by nurturing an outrage perpetrated against her forty years earlier. She feels that she has been victimized and she gives voice to her sense of victimization late in the novel when Rigaud threatens to expose her fraudulence. Attempting to justify her behavior she says:

> 'When, within a twelve-month of our marriage, I found my husband . . . to have sinned against the Lord and outraged me. . . . Was I to dismiss in a moment—not my own wrongs—what was I! but all the rejection of sin . . . in which I had been bred?'
>
> (II, 30, 844)

The key to her rationalization is her phrase "outraged me." She perceives herself to have been monstrously abused. She has been affronted by Mr. Clennam's lie. They had wed, according to their religious beliefs, in ostensible purity. She had obeyed religious stricture; he had not. One of her primary provisos of the marriage had been that Mr. Clennam be reared under the same religious doctrine as she, and her expectation was that he would hold that creed sacred. From her perspective Mr. Clennam had not only committed a gross violation against God's law, but he had shamelessly offended against her feelings.

In addition to her husband's offense against her, she has been outraged by her own body. She is barren, and she obliquely refers to that fact when she vengefully forces Arthur's mother to give him up to her. She says poignantly, " 'You have a child; I have none.' " This is an expression of her sense of marginality. Within the context of her Calvinist belief that she and all mankind are born into sin, she is marginal in relation to most of the other female sinners in the world. She is not fecund. According to her subconscious reasoning she must therefore be doubly sinful. If she is more sinful than the other sinners in her religion then she is marginal within her own religious subgroup. She believes herself to be doubly sinful or else why would God have made her barren?

In confronting Arthur's natural mother, Mrs. Clennam feels her inadequacy keenly. She cannot conceive a child; Arthur's mother can. Mrs. Clennam cannot even solace herself with the idea that it might have been Mr. Clennam's fault that they are childless, since he has been able to father a child on someone else. The blow to Mrs. Clennam's self-image must be vastly greater when she discovers that it is she, and not Mr. Clennam, who is sterile. In retaliation for her husband's sin and potency she jealously demands the issue of that potency for herself. In addition to being outraged by her husband and by her own body, she has been wounded by fate.

Mr. Clennam has an affair which is illegal and immoral and that union bears fruit. The union between Mr. Clennam and Mrs. Clennam which is legal and sanctioned by the church does not bear fruit. The moral marriage is, by an irony of fate, barren. Mrs. Clennam's insistence on taking the child from its natural mother may be due (in addition to revenge) to her hysterical determination to avenge herself on fate.

Mrs. Clennam is also appalled by Arthur's behavior on his return to England. Bitterly disappointed, she accepts his refusal to become her partner. Sorrowfully, she acknowledges his disregard for her aging and infirm condition. Pained, she reconciles herself to his insensitivity regarding her efforts at rapprochement. But she does not assent to his attack upon her self-image. His doubt about her integrity is an outrage she will not condone. She needs to appear righteous to Arthur. He is the only person who matters to her and he is accurately casting aspersions upon her honor.

From Mrs. Clennam's perspective, Arthur's accusations are poor rewards for her protection of him. She has invested in Arthur from his infancy, publicly shielding him from the shame of his birth, preventing his possible future indigence, and preparing him for a secure financial future. She has expended time, energy and a distorted nurturing on him (in the only way she understands mothering) and she does not receive in return the expected rewards of motherhood, even of motherhood once removed. To her that is an outrage. Whereas she has been a puritanically punitive parent, she has not been a neglectful one. Mrs. Clennam was available to Arthur to clothe, feed and educate him, albeit in her repressive fashion. In her guilt-ridden and fierce way she has some feeling of tenderness for Arthur. He is the only person, beside Flintwinch, with whom she has had a relationship of extended duration. Dickens presents her as a woman in comparative isolation, without a single friend. Arthur is her only link with a human impulse. She wants to share the House of Clennam with him. Although it is a decaying and defunct house, architecturally and financially, it is the only legacy she has to offer. The house is her essence. She and the house are inextricably co-mingled. When the house is subsequently consumed by fire, she is destroyed. She becomes completely catatonic. She symbolically turns to stone and never recovers from her hysterical paralysis.

Her earlier partial paralysis, which is a precursor to her final total paralysis, is in part a result of her sense of isolation and desolation. Her early immobilization occurs after she sends Arthur away to China, and she is left alone. She has sent him away in order to dissolve the engagement between him and Flora, but it is on one level a sacrifice. With Arthur gone she is totally isolated from family, having lived apart from her husband for many years. She lives completely alone but for the services of Flintwinch and Affery. She therefore has sufficient time to brood upon the outrages perpetrated against her, and to nurture them for forty years.

In order to keep her sense of victimization alive for so long a period of time she had to be very disciplined. Yet she used her resolve for destructive purposes. She initiated her spiteful punishment when Arthur was a child. She kept him in his father's presence as a daily reproach to Mr. Clennam. Currently, she keeps the watch on her desk as a daily reminder not to forget the past. She had, in the past, and continues in the present, to read the punitive portions of the bible daily, to help her to reinforce her determination to be vengeful. She is fearful of forgetting and uses these symbols to reinforce her painful recollections.

Describing the indignities of her early life she says:

'You do not know what it is . . . to be brought up strictly and straitly. . . . Mine was no light youth of sinful gaiety and pleasure. Mine were days of wholesome repression, punishment, and fear.'

(II, 30, 843)

Her words contain a double message. In addition to describing her heritage of moral values (which she subsequently ignores) she is indicating how hard and dour a life she has led. She describes her life, rationalizing it with pride but the words denote pain and indignity. The painful past which was perpetrated against her from childhood, and distortedly cloaked in the symbols of religion, initiated her into the misuse of religious symbols for destructive purposes.

She misuses symbols not only on religious and behavioral levels but also on a physiological plane. The punishment she has inflicted on herself is symbolic. Her paralysis has been from its inception a functional illness rather than a physiological one. It is inextricably connected with her subconscious sense of having been wounded in so many ways. Her paralysis operates on four planes. It serves to prevent her conscious awareness of the murderous rage she feels at having been outraged. It functions as a curb to the possibility of her acting out that murderous rage. It serves as a defense against her mental anguish and it provides a punishment for the guilt she bears for her immoral action against the Dorrits.

The proof that her paralysis is a hysterical immobilization is shown in her ability, prior to the fire, to overcome her infirmity and to rise up out of her wheelchair. She does so when Arthur's image of her is in jeopardy. She overcomes her paralysis to maintain her projected image of herself, as a righteous woman, in Arthur's eyes. But Arthur is never able to overcome his vague suspicion of his mother's dishonest conduct. Nor is he able to corroborate his fears about her dishonor. He is just left with an imprecise uneasiness about her morality.

Actually, Mrs. Clennam is incapable of providing any proof that would reinstate her honor in Arthur's eyes. She can not offer truth and its concomitant reparations without pressure from Rigaud. When she finally makes restitution to Amy, she does so only because Rigaud is threatening to expose her fraudulence. Her motivation in volunteering to repay her debt is not one of a revelatory nature. Her motive does not indicate sudden awareness of infamy and true repentance for it. Her incentive stems from her love for Arthur and her herculean effort to prevent him from knowing the truth about her character. The documents proving Mrs. Clennam's iniquity to Amy are in Amy's hands (as yet unopened). Mrs. Clennam, rising from her wheelchair, flees to Amy as a suppliant, kneeling before her and kissing the hem of Little Dorrit's dress. She begs for forgiveness which Amy freely bestows. In beseeching Amy not to reveal the truth to Arthur while Mrs. Clennam is still alive, she clearly states her reasons for wanting to shield him from the truth. She says:

> 'I would not, for any worldly recompense I can imagine, have him in a moment however blindly, throw me down from the station I have held before him all his life, and change me altogether, into something he would cast out of his respect. . . . Let me never feel, while I am still alive, that I die before his face, and utterly perish away from him.'
>
> (II, 31, 860)

In her hysterical and disconsolate speech Mrs. Clennam confesses a need for Arthur's respect and love that precludes monetary considerations. Despite her overweening pride she loves him. She has loved him throughout her long periods of isolation from him. She reveals that affection when, bemoaning his separation from her, she says to Amy: " 'With an empty place in his heart . . . he has turned away from me, and gone his separate road.' " Her perception of Arthur is accurate. There is a void in him, but Mrs. Clennam is also talking about the vacancy in her heart since he has abandoned her. In her grim and loveless life there is a particle of tender human emotion reserved for her adopted son. Nonetheless, Arthur's bleak background has impaired him and he leaves an imprint of pain on his mother and on the other significant characters with whom he interacts.

Amy and Arthur: Love and Pain

In his hero's relationship with his heroine, Dickens presents Arthur as a character who exhibits nobility of purpose in an ironically flawed manner. Arthur's actions are marred by insensitivity. His ethical concern is to rectify an injustice he suspects has been perpetrated against the Dorrits by the House of Clennam. However, in an effort to redress that wrong, Arthur is rude, intrusive and careless of Amy's feelings, blind to the conflict he adds to her life. The additional discord that Arthur introduces into Amy's world centers on two basic themes: her immediate economic survival and her eventual love for him. Arthur's behavior to her might easily place her job in jeopardy, and whereas he is attracted to her modesty, it takes him an inordinately long time to perceive her devotion to him.

Amy's shyness appears in direct contrast to Mrs. Clennam's authoritarianism, and may account for Arthur's immediate interest in the heroine when he notices her child-like form at the Clennam House. Passive in most interactions, Arthur's initial pursuit of Amy is aggressive. Her diffidence mirrors his and he sees a reflection of his inner self in her fragile exterior. In order to learn more about her history he follows her to the Marshalsea and intrudes upon her privacy.

Amy doesn't live in seclusion, but her place of residence is a secret she desperately wants to guard. She is wise enough to know that an employer might terminate her services if it were known that she lived in a jail. She is unaware that Mrs. Clennam, her employer, is privy to her background. Consequently, she flits unobtrusively from the Marshalsea to the Clennam establishment and back again to the jail while attempting to avoid detection.

Arthur, however, is insensitive to Amy's reserve. His curiosity about her is more important to him than Amy's implicit need for privacy. After he follows her to the Marshalsea, he gains access to William Dorrit's detention cell in order to satisfy his curiosity further. Arthur rationalizes his obtrusive actions, telling himself and Amy that his purpose in following her is to do her a service, but the result of his behavior humiliates and frightens her. She does not want to engage in secret conference with Arthur since it might given offense to Mrs. Clennam. She courteously but forthrightly tells Arthur how she feels when she says, " 'You are very good, sir. You speak very earnestly to me . . . but I wish you had not watched me.' " She explains her fear of losing her job, saying:

> 'Mrs. Clennam has been of great service to me; I don't know what we should have done without the employment she has given me; I am afraid it may not be a good return to become secret with her; I can say no more tonight, sir. I am sure you mean to be kind to us. Thank you, thank you.'
>
> (I, 8, 126)

Amy is aware of Arthur's intent to be of service and is, in part, courteously responding to it. Her polite behavior is also due to the fact that Arthur is her employer's son which places her in the embarrassing position of having to repulse his offer of friendship.

Because of the awkward position in which Arthur is placing her, Amy is telling him to desist. She is clearly stating that she cannot form a secret alliance with her employer's son regardless of his good intentions. She is telling him that his inquisitiveness is placing her job and her family's survival in danger. Nevertheless, Arthur ignores her discomfort and insists on staying. He demands to know more about her and continues to question her. Although Arthur seems impervious to Amy's discomfort and to her implicit request that he leave, he is actually aware of the distress his presence has engendered. Earlier he observed Amy's humiliation when Dorrit requested a "testimonial" from him. He perceived her anguish. He watched as she silently entreated her father to desist from his mendicancy and he thought that:

> To see her hand upon his arm in mute entreaty half-repressed, and her timid little shrinking figure turning away, was to see a sad, sad sight.
>
> (I, 8, 123)

Arthur has, throughout their encounter in the cell, and shortly thereafter in the courtyard, an element of compassion for Amy's anguish, but not sufficient empathy to ease her pain.

He is selfish and reacts with insensitivity to the fact that his presence was and continues to be a source of humiliation to her. He ignores the fact that although Dorrit humiliated Amy it was Arthur's uninvited presence there that triggered Dorrit's behavior. Arthur is impervious to the fact that Amy disappears from the cell as quickly as she can and runs into the courtyard to be alone. Arthur does not permit her the dignity of privacy but follows her into the courtyard and confronts her with questions. He wants to know how long she has known his mother, how she initially became acquainted with his mother, and whether his mother made the first overture to her.

Arthur wants information. The satisfaction of his curiosity is paramount to him. His desire for facts ignores Amy's "tremulous and agitated" need for privacy. He rationalizes that he is pursuing her for a moral purpose. He says, " 'Pray forgive me . . . I followed you . . . that I might endeavor to render you and your family some service.' " Nevertheless he is pinioning her to the spot against her wishes and he does not leave although she tactfully urges him to do so. He pursues his interrogation (which causes her pain and conflict) in the name of friendship.

Although Arthur's determination to unearth the truth has a moral impulse, there is an additional subconscious factor motivating his determined quest. His deeper motive relates to his resentful attitude toward Mrs. Clennam. He is obsessed with finding fault with his mother. If he can find a moral flaw in his mother he will be justified in not going into partnership with her. He has no positive goal to pursue, other than unearthing truth about his parents. He is unclear as to what he wants to do with his freedom. He has no occupation, no route that he wants to follow for a life's work, and he has sufficient time to brood obsessively about the possibility of his mother's nefarious practices. He rationalizes his obsession with a moral base and his determination to uncover his mother's iniquity becomes a moral obsession.

Arthur is correct in his suspicion, which is based solely on the slim nuances revealed to him on his father's deathbed. In his accurate assumption of chicanery, Arthur is a man with a keen but one-sided perception. He has insight into only one area, fraud. It is interesting to note that in all but the one area of knavery, Arthur is blind to nuance. He is oblivious of the love Amy feels for him as he has been blind to the love, in varying degrees, felt for him by Mrs. Clennam, Affery and Flora.

Arthur's dubiety regarding parental honesty fuels his actions and takes precedence over the pain he inflicts on Amy. Yet he is never successful in clarifying his doubts, nor in making restitution to Little Dorrit. He does become the instrument through which recompense is made, but it is accomplished by Mrs. Clennam. The reason his mother ultimately redresses the wrong done to Amy is that she loves her son and doesn't want him to know about her reprehensible behavior to the Dorrits. Justice is ironically served through Mrs. Clennam's love, not by Arthur's aggressive participation in the search for justice.

Although there is a moral impulse in Arthur's ineffectual probing, there is a destructive element in it as well. In addition to his meddlesomeness, which inflicts suffering on Amy, it is self-defeating, in that he wants to find his parents guilty of scandalous behavior. By discovery of parental infamy, he might thus assuage his own guilt for his abiding resentment of them.

Arthur's enduring indignation is evident upon his arrival at his mother's house. In a passive-aggressive gesture, he perversely visits her on the Sabbath, knowing that for Mrs. Clennam it is a sacred day reserved for solitary prayer. Greeted at the door by Flintwinch, who mentions Arthur's breach of sensibility, Arthur's response contains a reproof to the family retainer. " 'You wouldn't have me go away again?' " he asks, dismissing his own insensitivity. In effect, the old man is saying that Arthur has used poor judgment and has shown lack of respect in a matter of primary significance to his mother. However, Flintwinch bids him enter and informs him that his mother has been an invalid for fifteen years and is bedridden much of the time. Arthur makes no comment about his mother's condition, gives it no thought. Instead he bemoans his reception, although his arrival, long overdue, is unexpected. He muses:

> How weak am I . . . that I could shed tears at this reception! I, who have never experienced anything else; who have never expected anything else.
>
> (I, 31, 72)

Although he yearns for warmth from his mother, he has little compassion to spare for her. He is less concerned with pity for Mrs. Clennam than with self-pity.

Arthur's lack of empathy for his mother extends to his relationship with Amy. Although he commiserates with the latter, his sympathy is tainted with thoughtlessness. If Arthur really felt the sorrow for Amy that he thinks he feels, he would not continue to harass her. Although she has begged him not to pursue her nor to be secretive with her, he sends her a note after their initial encounter, asking that she meet him the following day at her uncle's house.

Amy's compliant response is motivated by two factors. She wants to thank Arthur for his generosity to Dorrit, and, more important, she wants to justify and excuse Dorrit's behavior to Arthur. She asks him not to misjudge her father, explaining that Dorrit has been in jail for so lengthy a period that he is no longer the man she is certain he was before his incarceration, and that even in his present situation he is courted and respected. In relieving her heart Amy elicits true compassion from Arthur. Although he sees that her fidelity to Dorrit has "shed false brightness round him," Arthur tells her that he will never think unjustly or harshly of Dorrit. Arthur's comforting response elicits, in turn, trust from Amy and she rescinds her previous comment that she wished Arthur had not followed her. Amy's agitation and tremulousness which were evident at the onset of this second meeting diminish, and her fear of Arthur lessens.

With the diminution of her fear of him, Arthur again takes up his investigative pursuit, questioning Little Dorrit about her father's creditors. Amy informs him that Tite Barnacle of the Circumlocution Office is the most influential of Dorrit's creditors. Arthur immediately proposes approaching Barnacle with a view to possibly terminating Dorrit's imprisonment. Amy acknowledges the hopelessness of such an endeavor, saying:

> 'Even if it could be done . . . and it never can be done . . . where would father live, or how could he live? I have often thought that if such a change could come, it might be anything but a service to him now. People might not think so well of him outside as they do there. He might not be so gently dealt with outside as he is there. He might not be so fit himself for the life outside, as he is for that'
>
> (I, 9, 139)

Prescient in the matter of her father's inability to cope with freedom, Amy is also divulging aspects of her own unconscious feeling in relation to her father and to freedom. She is inadvertently expressing her view of Mr. Dorrit's inappropriate behavior. She is also revealing her unexpressed fear of what would happen to her outside the walls. How would she live? What control would she have over the outside environment? What would her role become in relationship to her father? Amy cannot admit that she herself will not be so fit for life outside. In the deepest recesses of her soul she doesn't want Dorrit's restoration. She is prescient about Dorrit's inability to cope with freedom but she is not fully aware of her own limitations for a life beyond the Marshalsea.

Clennam as well as Dorrit is ineffectual in coping with freedom. Although he tries to assist Dorrit, he cannot transcend the Circumlocution Office. He is ineffectual in affecting Dorrit's release from the Marshalsea. When Dorrit is ultimately liberated from prison, it is not due to Arthur's intervention but to Pancks' investigative techniques. Arthur participates with Pancks in the investigation that eventually unearths a legacy to which the Dorrits are entitled, but it is Pancks, not Arthur, who discreetly collects the information relevant to Dorrit's freedom. When Pancks' data seem to be sufficiently promising to warrant the expectation of Dorrit's release, he informs Arthur of his findings and Arthur becomes an active participant in the successful venture.

There is a pattern to Arthur's incompetent behavior which appears in his relationship with Amy and which surfaces again in his relationship with Doyce. With purportedly kind intentions, Arthur causes distress. He rationalizes that he wants to be of service to Doyce, that he wishes to compensate Doyce for the years of harassment and humiliation inflicted on his partner by the Circumlocution Office. Nonetheless, his behavior results in the humiliation of bankruptcy for himself and for Doyce. Arthur is no more successful in his attempts to do Doyce a service than he is in his efforts to do Amy a service. He cannot compensate Doyce and he cannot recompense the Dorrits.

The pattern of Arthur's behavior is based on self-delusion. He devises satisfying yet semi-correct reasons for his motives and actions in dealing with Amy and with Doyce. His reasoning that he wishes to be of service has a kindly overtone to it, but beneath the surface Arthur is unconsciously reacting perversely to Doyce, as he reacted wilfully to Amy. Arthur is also being as contumacious with his partner as he had been with his mother. His bitter resentment toward his mother breeds an obstinacy which characterizes his relations with other people.

Mrs. Clennam wants Arthur to be her partner. Arthur obstinately refuses. He doesn't heed her. Later in the novel, Doyce expects that Arthur will not speculate. Arthur disregards his partner; he doesn't attend to him. Arthur is subconsciously projecting the image of his mother's firm, into which he was expected to enter as a partner, onto the one in which he is actually a partner. He is inadvertantly interweaving both firms into one. He is being obdurate and perverse to a partner who, unlike his mother, never harmed him. He is not seeing clearly. He is unaware of the psychological impulse which partially motivates his business action. Ultimately he pays the penalty for his lack of awareness and for his unethical behavior.

What is in fact unethical in Arthur's actions is his disregard of the unwritten contract between him and Doyce. Their moral agreement is that Arthur will not play the stock market. They discuss the subject before Doyce leaves for France to patent his invention. He and Arthur engage in a discussion in which Arthur corroborates Doyce's objection to gambling on the stock market. Doyce refers to his objection as a "prejudice." Arthur soothingly responds by saying " 'But you shouldn't call it a prejudice. . . . My dear Doyce, it is the soundest sense,' " adding that speculation is a folly deserving the name of vice.

Although Arthur does not specifically state that he will not speculate, he leads Doyce to believe that he won't. By his responsiveness to Doyce's feelings on the subject, Doyce has every reason to assume that his wishes will be honored. An honorable man himself, he has no reason to doubt his partner's future behavior in this matter. The ethical assumption there-fore, is that their verbal agreement will be honored. For Arthur to ignore the intent and injunction of Doyce's wishes, is to be, if not unethical, at least secretive and underhanded. Arthur does not openly rediscuss the topic with Doyce and signify his intention to speculate. He gambles secretively. By not honoring his verbal contract with Doyce, Arthur is engaging in a fraud-ulent act.

It is interesting to note that fraudulence is the predominant idea in Arthur's mind. He is concerned with his mother's deceit and Amy's victimization from it, yet the deceptive act he engages in is also a fraudulent act which victimizes Doyce. Arthur is attracted to and repelled by fraudulence and therefore he has chosen to ignore the trust placed in him by his partner.

Arthur's blindness to his own motivations and his disregard for other people's wishes are seen in his insensibility to love, and to the pain his lack of perception causes. He is unaware that he is in love with Little Dorrit and equally unaware that she is in love with him. In his lack of sensibility to the developing interaction between them, he inflicts pain on the one person for whom he experiences a sense of compassion.

Solicitous and sorrowing thoughts of Little Dorrit have remained with Arthur from the first night he met her. He has had visions of her malnourished face which have led him to the unhappy but accurate conclusion that she has suffered from "years of insufficient food, if not want." The sorrow he has experienced is, in part, a symbolic projection of his own deprivations. He has anguished over an inadequate supply of love and insufficiency of warmth in his emotional life. However, despite his concern for Amy, he continues to afflict her. He has initially caused her pain because of his lack of sensitivity to her fears. Later on in the novel he distresses her by his obtuseness to her feelings for him. He induces sorrow when he tells her how he fancied that once, long ago, he had loved someone, but that tender emotion is no longer possible at his age. He has no idea that his words are unbearable for Amy to hear, but merely wonders why he is unburdening his heart to her.

Amy tries unsuccessfully to awaken a mutual response of love from him. She wants to indicate her feeling in a delicate manner. She speaks to him with a poignant pleading that announces her affection if he would but see it. She patiently explains why he has been unburdening himself, saying:

> 'Because you trust me, I hope. Because you know that nothing can touch you, without touching me; that nothing can make you happy or unhappy, but it must make me, who am so grateful to you, the same.'
>
> (I, 32, 433)

Arthur hears and sees all the signs of devotion emanating from her; the keen emotion in her voice, the earnest gaze upon her face, the quickened heaving of her breast, but "the remotest suspicion of the truth never dawned upon his mind." He sees her only as a deprived child-heroine, slender in body, strong in soul. Arthur remains blind to Amy's love for him and her attendant suffering, due to his obtuseness. He remains impervious to her love for him until his incarceration, at which point Young John Chivery informs Arthur of Amy's feeling for him. Arthur's self-deprecating reaction to the information is one of uncomprehending bewilderment. He is stupefied by the intelligence. "Consider the improbability," he ponders, at some length. Dazed by this turn of events he begins to question at last whether or not he has ever tentatively viewed in "half-formed consciousness" the hope that she might care for him. He finally comes to the realization that his feeling of compassion for her and her expressions of gratitude to him both contain the tender element of love. Nevertheless, he deprecates the possibility of their love ever coming to fruition because of his age and immurement.

During his imprisonment for bankruptcy, Arthur pines in the old cell in the Marshalsea that was once William Dorrit's. Noting Arthur's melancholy while tending him, Amy observes as she did with Dorrit that "the shadow of the wall was dark upon him." She attempts to provide the succor to Arthur that she once ministered to Dorrit. She brings him flowers, attends to his nourishment and reads to him. She reads aloud in an effort to comfort him, but Arthur is inconsolable. Dickens describes the ennervating effect that the ambience of prison has on life. The Marshalsea wore its "changeless and barren" look. "Blossom what would, its brick and bars wore uniformly the same dead crop." Dickens uses the physical laws of nature and the intellectual processes of the mind (the autumnal flowering of plants and the blossoming of the intellect in the reading process) to create a metaphor for the deadening toll imprisonment takes on its occupants. Neither nature nor the mind of man can efface the effect of the Marshalsea's ambience and architecture on Amy and Arthur.

Arthur's depression and his fallacious conception of his unworthiness to be loved, in conjunction with his misperception of Amy's current superior station in life, cause him to suggest a separation from Little Dorrit. However, Amy will not permit herself to be disjoined. Although Arthur has inadvertently caused her emotional turmoil, she loves him and wants to maintain their relationship. The suffering she has endured causes her to manipulate the scene in the jail in which she proposes marriage to Arthur. Amidst her tender loving care of him, she exhibits one of her weaknesses. Dickens insures that the reader will not forget that Amy is human, that she is not an angel, and that she is a character whose suffering has left scars. Amy behaves with Arthur similarly to the way she conducted herself with Maggy. She deceives Arthur into thinking she has enormous wealth although in so doing she is causing him pain. " 'Do you feel quite stong enough to know what a great fortune I have got?' " When Arthur answers in the affirmative she, knowing his response in advance, asks if he will accept it. Arthur's retort is a vehement negative. After many deceitfully ambiguous remarks which tend to corroborate Arthur's anguished misperception that Amy is currently too rich for him to consider as a marriage partner, at last the heroine discloses that she too is penniless.

What Little Dorrit has done in toying with Arthur's emotions in his dejected and vulnerable state, is analagous to the hoax she perpetrated against Maggy when she pretended to secure a night's lodging for the weary grotesque. The "pious fraud" Amy perpetrates against Arthur is incorporated into the end of the novel because Dickens wants the reader to remember that Amy is a human heroine, not a saintly one.

To this end, Dickens reinforces, in the jail scene, a variation of the provocative pattern of behavior Amy engages in in an effort to exercise control over the unsatisfying conditions of her life. Dickens wants the reader to recall the events Amy is remembering and to feel vicariously the pain she has suffered in her association with Arthur. His insensitive behavior induces her to tease him in subconscious retaliation for the afflictions he has imposed upon her. Incorporated in her disquietude is Arthur's previous rejection of her avowal of affection. Furthermore, she has no assurance that he will accept that which he previously spurned. He might dismiss her current overture as he has ignored prior expressions of love from her. Added to her anxiety is the knowledge that he has loved others, but considers himself presently too old for so tender an emotion. All of these doubts conspire to create a presentation of her loving intent that has fear as its base and an element of aggression in it that cloaks her apprehension, which is released via the teasing.

In addition to her dread of rejection, Amy is motivated by another terror. She fears lonesomeness. With the deaths of her father and uncle, and with Fanny's marriage to Sparkler, Amy, but for Arthur is condemned to excrutiating loneliness. Although she loves Arthur, these are the human factors which contribute to the short-lived pain she inflicts on him. Dickens does not want the reader to forget that his heroine has been unduly tormented in her relationship with his unheroic hero. Arthur's prolonged blindness to her romantic interest in him has wounded her deeply, and if she exhibits a mild hostility in her teasing of him, she may be pardoned. Dickens does not intimate that Amy will live happily ever after, rather that she will continue to have her sorrows intermingled with modest joy. That is the reason Dickens ends his darkest and most pessimistic novel with the bride and groom walking away from the church "in sunshine and shade." The placement of the noun signifying comparative darkness at the end of the phrase is intended to linger and reverberate in the reader's consciousness. Shade conjures shadow and the latter is Dickens' reminder that the shadow of the Marshalsea cannot be expunged from Amy's and Arthur's history. Although the protagonists are partially irradiated by the love and happiness that sunshine connotes, they are also lastingly subject to the gloom and obscurity that diminished light signifies. Through his realistically portrayed protagonists, Dickens is saying that there is but miniscule certainty for happiness in the world as it is constituted, and that the despairing condition of human life is everybody's fault, a theme Dickens ironically incorporated into the novel's original title: *Nobody's Fault.*

5

Conclusion

It is the premise of this book that Dickens' theme of deception and its presentation in narrative and characterization cohere to form the intense unity of *Little Dorrit*. Duplicity, the essence of the narrative which articulates the subject matter, is the organizing principle of Dickens' novel of imprisonment. Central to my study is a minute examination of the dualities inherent in Dickens' presentation.

Dickens' dissimulating narrative relies on techniques calculated to lead the reader into errors of judgment. His method consists of stratagems that betray the reader into accepting surface impressions of his most important characters. His scrupulous attention to detail overwhelms the reader with stimuli in order to conceal the equivocal nature of his representations of Amy, Arthur, Fanny, Mrs. Clennam, Flora and Mr. F's Aunt. Dickens' ambiguous portrayal of these six characters is a departure in style from his presentation of the remaining cast of *Little Dorrit*, and this purposeful inconsistency in portraiture is part of his devious strategy. Since most of the cast is easily subject to familiar classification, the reader has a reasonable tendency to so regard these six individuals. However, careful scrutiny of the six reveals paradoxes and equivocations of characterization which their initial impressions contradict. Repeated close readings uncover the significance of the essential roles that the six characters play in unifying this masterpiece of Dickens' maturity.

Although modern criticism has enhanced our awareness of Dickens' consummate artistry in *Little Dorrit*, many critics maintain a traditional perspective regarding these six individuals. It is a commonplace that Amy is servile, Arthur obtuse, Fanny wrathful, Mr. F's Aunt comedic, Flora silly and Mrs. Clennam vindictive. My study has brought forward equally significant qualities of hostility in Amy, obstinacy in Arthur, love in Fanny, empathy in Mr. F's Aunt, resentment in Flora and vulnerability in Mrs. Clennam. The aforementioned traits surface when the characters' superficial images are pierced. Amy's submissiveness cloaks her passive aggression. Arthur's perversity masquerades under the guise of kindness. Fanny's sisterly love emerges beneath her rage. Mrs. Clennam's frigidity masks her longing for filial affection. Flora's loquacity conceals her rancor. And Mr. F's Aunt's hostility shrouds her identity as Flora's alter ego. Although positive emotions issue in some of the characters where none were thought to exist, and negative feelings arise in characters where only positive traits have been noticed, the preponderant tone of the novel is one of hostility. Notwithstanding the fact that Flora and Mr. F's Aunt are comedic representations, they serve an important function in carrying forward the theme of hostility which pervades the novel and is one of its unifying elements.

The tone of belligerence which permeates *Little Dorrit* bears a resemblance to the feelings of antagonism which Dickens reveals in his personal correspondence. An additional aim of this study has been to correlate the negative emotions that Dickens' letters disclose, to similar qualities in the novel. Dickens' humiliation of his wife is reflected in Dorrit's abasement of Amy and the author's insensitivity to Kate surfaces in the hero's callousness toward the heroine. The extent of the correlation between Dickens' disagreeable traits and those found in certain characters in *Little Dorrit* has been, but for the exceptions noted elsewhere in this study, mainly ignored in the critical canon.

As I have demonstrated, the prevailing view of Amy Dorrit as a sainted heroine is an image that the novel does not sustain, and is one that should be abandoned in order to apprehend the extent of psychological realism with which she has been drawn. Dickens' correspondence has shown that he is not impervious to the exacting demands made on Victorian women. Nor is he unmindful of their damaging consequences. He is aware of binary oppositions in humans, no more so than in his representation of Amy and the other important characters in *Little Dorrit*. In his understanding of the enduring psychological and environmental influences on personality, Dickens soundly provides no major transformations in the characters, except for the conversion from bitterness to acceptance in the comedic Flora Finching.

In Dickens' uncommon portrait of the protagonist in *Little Dorrit*, the impelling quest for artistic verity may have subconsciously been a determinant, superseding Dickens' personal views regarding femininity. With Amy, Dickens is moving toward a modern twentieth century realism in character portrayal. Among his heroines, Amy is an anomaly. No other Dickens' heroine is so dedicated to performing the grueling functions of a female victim, yet so passively aggressive, manipulative and deceitful in carrying out those tasks. In his artful portrayal of her, Dickens is showing Amy's psychological mechanisms for survival in untenable circumstances.

Dickens advances further in his movement toward psychological modernity with his comprehension of the lasting effects of early, and or, prolonged victimization. Dickens astutely assesses the difficulties inherent in liberation after years of emotional and physical imprisonment, not only with Amy but with William Dorrit as well. In their centrality to the novel, Dickens shows father and daughter suffering from the disequilibrium of success after years of habituated want. Neither gender can make the transition from victimization to liberation. The security system of father and daughter alike is endangered when they are released from confinement and poverty. Each lacks familiarity with freedom and prosperity.

Amy and her father symbolically reflect Dickens' early emotional history—the pain of his youthful drudgery at Warren's Blacking, his father's incarceration, young Charles' removal from his beloved grammar school, the loss of his sister's closeness and his isolation from the family. These childhood memories are mirrored in the sorrow, loneliness and alienation seen in *Little Dorrit*. To some extent, the man and the artist can be observed in his mid-forties attempting to expiate these childhood deprivations, in addition to trying to cope with disillusionment, macrocosmically, with the state of the world and microcosmically, with the state of his marriage. Dickens' dissatisfaction with life, despite his extraordinary achievements, can be seen in the frenzied social, civic and literary activities in which he engaged during the writing of *Little Dorrit*. We cannot know with assuredness what Dickens was feeling, but we can reasonably postulate from evidence in the text and in the letters that he appears to have been an angry and embittered man (at this juncture in his life) trying to fight his way out of a depression through activity. This supposition is bolstered by the fact that Dickens did succumb to depression upon the completion of *Little Dorrit*.

Dickens' disenchanted vision of the world is also apparent in his philosophical attitude toward the rewards of virtue. His concern with recompense for moral behavior is illustrated by his rendering of the most exemplary family in *Little Dorrit*, the Plornishes. These minor characters reinforce Dickens' dubiety about Victorian morality. The Plornishes give food on credit to their less fortunate neighbors. Whereas this action is intended to disclose the Plornishes' goodness, which it does, Dickens also asks the reader to ponder the effect of the Plornishes' integrity. What Dickens is actually saying is that the Plornishes will ultimately become impoverished since free enterprise requires that commodities be paid for. The inference is that they will be unable to stave off their own creditors and will ultimately be incarcerated for debt. The impending disastrous consequences of their generous impulse conjures an image of the Marshalsea, carrying forward the prevailing social symbol of the novel. In a wittingly deceitful manner, Dickens argues that virtue cannot sustain itself in Victorian society.

Dickens' unique treatment of the theme of deceit raises an interesting question. Why does subterfuge transcend plot and characterization to emerge as the essence of narrative strategy in *Little Dorrit?* Although commentators have ignored this query, the dismal picture of English life which *Little Dorrit* presents has caused many critics to look for an explanation of Dickens' dark vision by examining his personal history, and they have generally focused their attention on some of the incidents in his life that might account for the darkness of *Little Dorrit*.

In "Dickens: The Two Scrooges," (1940), Edmund Wilson notes the onset of Dickens' deep discontent at this period and postulates that the novelist experienced a serious anxiety about his artistic prowess for the first time in his life. In *Charles Dickens: His Tragedy and Triumph* (1952) Edgar Johnson observes the increased and unappeasable restlessness which marked Dickens' behavior in the eighteen-fifties and further, that Dickens underwent extraordinary difficulty in the writing of *Little Dorrit*. The problem of Dickens' and others' creativity is addressed in Elliot Jacques' psychoanalytic study of genius, *Death and the Mid-Life Crisis* (1965). Jacques contends that the artist's creativity is intense and comparatively effortless during his twenties and thirties, but that in mid-life, the pace slows and a "decisive change in the quality and content of creativity" takes place.

Dickens' singular use of subterfuge in *Little Dorrit* may have been partially due (as Jacques suggests) to the novelist's chronological maturation. However, other eminent commentators have brought forward equally compelling suppositions for Dickens' difficulties during the mid-eighteen hundreds. Malcom Y. Andrews properly reminds us in *Charles Dickens: The Public Readings* (1979), that Dickens was a popular entertainer as well as an artist and that the "means of sustaining popularity are seldom compatible with the slow cultivation of a subtler artistry. . . ."

It is not unreasonable to theorize that Dickens may have also been concerned and therefore partially motivated by some of the adverse criticism to which *Bleak House* (1852) and *Hard Times* (1854) were subject. The preceding novels (akin to *Little Dorrit*) were indictments of society, and the two prior works were accused of being deficient in humor. Dickens' artful presentation of deceit in the 1855-7 novel, may have been the result of his desire to maintain his popularity and simultaneously to prove to himself, and to his alert readers, that his artistic powers were not waning. If Wilson's theory is correct, that Dickens experienced concern about his creativity, *Little Dorrit* represented a creative challenge to the novelist in terms of his ability to express strong feelings of negativism with impunity. He allows Mr. F's Aunt to divulge her animosity under the guise of eccentricity. He permits himself to disclose his hostility to the world under the ruse of representing the condition of English life.

In *Dickens: A Life* (1979), the MacKenzies record that Dickens was a very angry man, easily enraged in business negotiations, political matters and in personal interactions with family and friends. The structure of hostility on which *Little Dorrit* is founded has its counterpart in the rage we can surmise Dickens to have felt at being middle-aged, unhappy at home and unable to achieve tranquility. His fear of waning creativity must have been somewhat assuaged by his creative capacity to transpose negative personal feelings into a complex art and still preserve his popular appeal.

Dickens' most recent biographer, Michael Slater, states in *Dickens and Women* (1983) that the novelist has a predilection for "exposing his deepest feelings to his beloved public without that public's at all suspecting what it is that he is doing." Slater also records Dickens' poignant explanation for his frenzied activities during 1853–7. The novelist writes that they were an attempt " 'to get by some means at some change that should make existence easier.' " In his misdirected effort to diminish despair, engaging in a method that could, at best, offer temporary respite, Dickens reveals an understandably self-delusory trait.

Certainly each of the traumatic events enumerated must have played a contributory role in shaping Dickens' negative world view during this period. However, since *Little Dorrit* is a singular work of deception in all of its component parts, it may well have been the literary vehicle through which Dickens was attempting to expiate or to justify his own self-deceptive tendencies. With all of his pressing problems during this trying period, it seems a reasonable postulation that Dickens, the individual, inseparable at times from Dickens the author, was trying to work out his emotional problems via his artistry with *Little Dorrit*.

Dickens' sly questioning of the rewards of virtue, his deceptive character representations and his misleading narrative technique combine to create a profoundly artistic work, one which requires repeated readings in order to be fully comprehended. The ambiguities that I have analyzed in *Little Dorrit* represent, I believe, a paradigm of Dickens' deceptive narrative strategy. Several additional conclusions seem pertinant to this study of the uniquely duplicitous quality of *Little Dorrit*. First, that by the magnitude of its artifice this novel occupies a special place in the canon. Second, that although it is distinctive in its presentation of guile, it nonetheless reinforces the unity of the canon since decepetion is a recurrent theme throughout Dickens' fiction. Third, that the themes of submerged hostility and deceit which permeate this work in fact reflect its essential driving impulse and significantly color its tone. A supplementary conclusion advances a theory in response to the central question logically arising from this study: Why is *Little Dorrit* so singularly misleading?

The artful presentation of deceit in *Little Dorrit* serves complicated purposes, fulfilling artistic, psychological and practical needs for Dickens. On an artistic level, his devious narrative strategies enhance characterization by revealing the conflicting forces which motivate the behavior of his six specially ambiguous portraits. On a psychological plane, his cunning techniques may have supplied proof to Dickens that his creative powers had not, as he seems to have felt, lessened. On a practical level, paradoxically, his indirection in *Little Dorrit* mitigates the possibility of the ordinary reader fully comprehending Dickens' hostility toward his society and therefore protects him against the risk of diminished popularity. If

Dickens' rage about personal relationships were to be recognized, or his dubiety about the rewards of virtue were fully understood, or his creation of a hero and heroine with realistically negative traits were completely comprehended, Dickens might reasonably have lost some of his popular appeal. And Dickens was equally concerned with the revenues that had accrued to him from a loyal public as well as with the self-satisfaction attendant upon positive literary criticism of his work. The deceptive quality of *Little Dorrit*, therefore, functions in a triple capacity for Dickens, accommodating his creative, emotional and financial needs during a period of his life we know to have been one of unappeasable restlessness and distress.

One of the reasons that many readers have closed this novel with an understandable sense of disquiet is that they have come to Dickens with preconceptions regarding his reverence for certain Victorian ideals. *Little Dorrit* undermines those anticipations, and offers instead contradictory messages whose function is to confound. Whereas Dickens presents aspects of the Victorian exemplar, he subverts the existing standard, since he realizes on some level of awareness, that it does not work. He decries duplicity, yet represents all humankind as deceitful. He observes societal myths and their concommitant paradoxes to which he can find no satisfactory solutions. In effect, what Dickens has done in this relentlessly grim novel has been to thwart his public's great expectations. Admiring readers have thought to become engrossed in familiar Victoriana; they have been confronted instead by alienating modernity. Dickens could not have forseen how apropos this novel would become to future centuries, yet *Little Dorrit* aptly speaks to our modern technological era, an age that induces loneliness and alienation, and that likewise sees greed, hypocrisy and chicanery flourish in all strata of society.

Appendix

Dickens' concern with Victorian standards of morality is further illustrated by an ambiguous sentence in *Little Dorrit*, whose sly significance has been mainly overlooked in the critical canon. Part of the author's dichotomous presentation appears in a crucial line in which he ironically measures Amy's virtue against the prototype of a young woman of antiquity. He writes: "There was a classical daughter once—perhaps—who ministered to her father in prison as her mother had ministered to her" (I, 19, 272–3). Dickens makes no mention of the classical daughter's name, but his reference to her raises some interesting questions. Who is she? What is her relevance to *Little Dorrit*? And how did Dickens know about her?

In order to evaluate the importance of Dickens' reference to the classical daughter, it is necessary to unearth her identity. Holloway (1967) identifies her as Euphrasia, daughter of the imprisoned King Evander of Syracuse, whom Euphrasia "fed with the milk of her breasts."[1] Holloway doesn't cite the source of his identification, so the reader cannot be sure of Euphrasia's identity, nationality, or the actuality of her existence. Hobhouse (1818) alludes to her as "the Roman daughter,"[2] without indicating her name. Murphy (1772), calling her "The Grecian Daughter,"[3] increases the ambiguities concerning her identity. None of the numerous dictionaries consulted on Greek and Roman mythology list the name Euphrasia. King Evander, however, is cited in the *Dictionary of Greek and Roman Biography and Mythology* (1967). Using Virgil's *Aenid* as its source, the *Dictionary* states that the monarch Evander had a son, Pallas and two daughters, neither of whom is named Euphrasia. The daughters are identified as Rome and Dyna.[4]

In antiquity, the name Euphrasia remains dubious, but the tale of the "pious" daughter perseveres in the literature. Hobhouse attempts to clarify the story by citing similar accounts of it in Festus and Solinus. But the contradictions proliferate. Hobhouse states that "The father in Festus is a mother in Pliny, and the plebian of the latter is a noble matron in Valerius Maximus."

A Temple of Piety, consecrated on a spot where the "pious" daughter was thought to have lived, produces further inconsistencies. The antiquaries do not agree on the location for the Temple, nor on the site of the prison housing the legendary Evander. Some of the ancients cite not one, but three Temples, built in the Forum Olitorium, the vestiges of which Hobhouse records. In an archeological approach, Hobhouse refers to the remains of lateral walls and Temple columns in the Forum in an attempt to determine if the Temple and the dungeon actually existed.

Although nothing definitive about the prison or Euphrasia is revealed by Hobhouse's study of the dungeon site, the text is valuable for its reflection of early nineteenth-century moral attitudes. Hobhouse's emphasis on filial piety is marked in the concluding lines of his notes on the "pious" daughter. He states that the nineteenth century has been furnished with a new piety, the "courageous attachment of wives to their husbands, under calamity." Such heroic devotion has always existed, Hobhouse observes, but has often gone unrecorded. The attachment of Euphrasia to Evander is analogous to Amy's devotion to William. We can therefore deduce, with some certainty, that Holloway is correct in assuming that Euphrasia is the character to whom Dickens is alluding. Yet the problem remains regarding the source of Dickens' knowledge of her.

There is reasonable evidence that Dickens was familiar with the tale, either in its written or dramatic form (possibly in both). As a tragedy, *The Grecian Daughter* was performed many times in London during the eighteen-thirties.[5] It is a commonplace that Dickens was an avid theatre-goer, frequenting Covent Garden, Drury Lane and the Haymarket, so it is a logical assumption that he saw the play.

An additional clue to the probability of Dickens' familiarity with the classical daughter is provided by Johnson's biography of Dickens. Johnson (1952) states that in September of 1841, Dickens had been discussing Byron's *Childe Harold's Pilgrimage*, and had written a parody on one of the stanzas. Although the stanza Dickens satirized does not refer to Euphrasia, it is not unreasonable to suppose that Dickens read the poem in its entirety. He would therefore have come across Canto IV, stanzas 148–151. These lines in Byron depict an elderly man imprisoned in a dungeon. He is attended by his daughter, who nourishes him with the milk from her breasts. This suckling image is what Dickens is referring to when he declares in his narrative that the classical daughter ministered to her father as her mother had ministered to her.

Nineteenth-century positions on Euphrasia's act of suckling her father vary. Hobhouse's glorification of Euphrasia's piety does not completely reflect nineteenth-century criticism of *The Grecian Daughter*. W. Oxberry (1822) expresses a divergent view. Commenting on Euphrasia's nursing of her father, Oxberry states that "if it does not deserve censure, [it] most assuredly does not permit praise."[6] John Galt (1831) remarks of the play that it is merely a set piece which aspiring young actresses "think necessary to go through before they consider their reputations established."[7] However, Jesse Foot (1811) mirrors the popular view of the tragedy which eighteenth-century audiences held. He states that *The Grecian Daughter* "bids fairer for longevity than any other modern drama whatever."[8]

The Grecian Daughter, Murphy's most popular tragedy, reduced eighteenth-century audiences to tears. Murphy presents Euphrasia as a self-sacrificing, dutiful daughter whose method of saving her father from starvation is considered an ultimate act of filial piety. Hester Lynch Piozzi (1794) observes that Euphrasia personified "the noblest example of womanhood."[9]

"W.S.," a contributor to *The Monthly Mirror* (1798), proclaims Euphrasia a most "amiable character."[10] *The London Chronicle* (1772), remarking on Euphrasia's nobility, adds that the play "possesses a very eminent degree of merit."[11]

However, in the nineteenth century the critical tide of eighteenth-century acclaim begins to turn, and by the twentieth century, Alardyce Nicoll (1927) finds the play dull.[12] Howard Dunbar (1946) observes that critics have "little to say of the tragedy."[13] And John Pike Emery (1946) states that Murphy "furnishes some novelty . . . by the omission of sexual love in . . . *The Grecian Daughter*."[14] Emery misreads the play. He does not comprehend the questionable morality of Euphrasia's suckling act, nor does he discern the incestuous implications of her ministrations.

For the modern reader, critical response to Murphy's play seems ill-defined. Excepting Oxberry's reproof in 1822, and Dickens' subsequent derision of the heroine, no reviewer questions the legitimacy of Euphrasia's action. Surprisingly, no one addresses the incestuousness inherent in the drama's theme. Equally problematic is the public's acceptance of the tragedy. Although the preponderance of Murphy's productivity is comedic or farcical, eighteenth-century audiences heralded the drama as a successful departure in style from Murphy's usual mode of writing. Moreover, exempting Oxberry and Dickens, nineteenth and twentieth-century detractors dismiss the play, one that enshrines female victimization, for trivial reasons. In the mid-twentieth century male and female critics alike neglect to articulate the reprehensibility of the drama's underlying message in its exploitative dimension of female devotion. Dickens, however, perceives the sexual nuances in Euphrasia's piety, and with customary irony, challenges her actions by a comparison of her with his own heroine. In the paragraph in which he mentions the classical daughter, he writes: "Little Dorrit, though of unheroic modern stock, and mere English, did much more in comforting her [father]."

Dickens' comments embody numerous levels of meaning.

First, in saying that Amy is of unheroic modern stock, he is deriding the heroism of Euphrasia and obliquely reminding the reader of Little Dorrit's humanly negative traits. Second, by terming Amy mere English, he is ironically implying a difference in standards of morality for heroines. He is indicating that an English heroine does not suckle her father. Third, in signifying that Amy gives more comfort than Euphrasia, he is making reference to Amy's drudgery, and once again casting doubt on Euphrasia's action as the ultimate manifestation of filial devotion. Consequently, Dickens is undermining the predominant eighteenth-century view of the Grecian daughter as "the noblest example of womanhood." Fourth, by his use of the analogy between the characters, Dickens is pointing toward a moral standard of relative virtue. He is indicating that by comparison with the classical daughter, Amy exhibits honorable restraint. In addition, the homology functions to alert the attentive reader to Amy's sexual (though unconsummated) desire for Dorrit. If such was not Dickens' aim, he would not have embodied in *Little Dorrit* a reference to a classical daughter whose dutifulness includes the dubious act of suckling her father. He would have omitted mention of Euphrasia, or he would have elected a less sexually ambiguous character for comparison with his heroine.

Little Dorrit illustrates the predicament of the Victorian female. Nineteenth-century standards for a woman place her in an untenable position, which Amy's situation exemplifies. In prison she is confronted with the lure of incest by her confinement in close quarters; in Europe she must contend with the meaninglessness of indolence contingent upon wealth. The paradox with which Dickens attempts to deal regarding society's expectations for women is represented by his dual acceptance and rejection of mid-Victorian dictates that severely limit women's options. Incorporating an allusion to the classical daughter into *Little Dorrit* serves to highlight his heroine's plight. Furthermore, in subtle elaboration of his philosophically transitional and understandably dichotomous world view, Dickens' comment on the Grecian father and daughter in a dungeon evokes echoes of the novelist's somber vision of existence. From the Greeks to the Victorians, the reverberating image in *Little Dorrit* is one of humankind in fettered condition.

Notes

[1] John Holloway, ed., Notes, *Little Dorrit* by Charles Dickens (New York: Penguin, 1967), p. 905.

[2] John Hobhouse, *Historical Illustrations of The Fourth Canto of Childe Harold* (London: Murray, 1818), p. 295.

[3] Arthur Murphy, "The Grecian Daughter," *The New English Drama* (London: Simpkin and Marshall, 1822). There's a good likelihood that Holloway got his source from Murphy's lines: "The father fostered at his daughter's breast O! filial piety!" p. 243.

[4] *Dictionary of Greek and Roman Biography and Mythology*, ed. William Smith (New York: AMS, 1967), II, 59. Neither Euphrasia nor Evander is cited in: (a) The *Oxford Classical Dictionary*, eds. Hammond and Sculard (Oxford: Clarendon, 1970); (b) *Le Petit Robert: Dictionnaire Universal Des Noms Propres*, ed. Paul Robert (Paris: SNL-Le Robert 2, 1977); (c) Paulys, *Realencyclopädie der Classischen Altertumswissenschaft* (Stuttgart: Metzlersche Buchhandlung, 1909), Vol. 6. Euphrasia is not listed as a proper noun but is cited as a common noun in two volumes: (a) *A Greek-English Lexicon* (1843; rpt. Oxford: Clarendon, 1958), p. 62; (b) Joseph T. Shipley, *The Dictionary of Word Origins* (New York: Philosophical Library, 1945), p. 144. In the former, euphrasia means "good cheer." In the latter it is defined as a verb meaning "to delight" or "to gladden" and is Hebraic in origin.

[5] Martin Meisel, *Realizations: Narrative, Pictorial, and Theatrical Arts in Nineteenth-Century England* (Princeton: Princeton UP, 1983. See also the *Catalogue of the Theatre and Drama Collections* (Boston: Hall, 1976), Part III: Non-Book Collection, 12, 50–1. *The Grecian Daughter* (1772) by Arthur Murphy, performed at the: (a) Theatre Royal, Covent Garden, 25 October, 1830, with Miss Fanny Kemble in the role of Euphrasia; (b) at Covent Garden, 1 February 1830, with Fanny Kemble; (c) at Covent Garden, 27 December 1830; (d) programmes for additional performances in 1830, starring Fanny Kemble as Euphrasia, omit the specific date; (e) further performances, minus specific dates, are recorded for the year 1832; (f) a reprint of an 1830 engraving of Fanny Kemble in the role of Euphrasia is included at the end of the appendix.

[6] W. Oxberry, *The New English Drama* (London: Simpkin and Marshall, 1822), p. 2.

[7] John Galt, *The Lives of the Players* (London: Colburn and Bentley, 1831), II, 125.

[8] Jesse Foot, "Literary Selections and Retrospect," *The New Annual Register*,

or *General Repository of History, Politics, and Literature, for the Year 1811* (London: Stockdale, 1812), p. 357.

9 Hester Lynch Piozzi, *British Symphony* (London: Robinson, 1794), I, 42.

10 "W.S.," "Biographical Sketch of Arthur Murphy, Esq.," *Monthly Mirror*, Dec. 1798, 6, 331.

11 "Theatrical Intelligence," *The London Chronicle*, February 1772, 31, 200.

12 Alardyce Nicoll, *A History of Late Eighteenth Century Drama: 1750-1800* (Cambridge: Univ. Press, 1927), p. 76.

13 H.H. Dunbar, *The Dramatic Career of Arthur Murphy* (New York: MLA, 1946), pp. 218–222.

14 John Pike Emery, *Arthur Murphy: An Eminent English Dramatist of the Eighteenth Century* (Philadelphia: Univ. of Pennsylvania Press, 1946), pp. 173–4.

MISS FANNY KEMBLE as EUPHRASIA.

PUB. MARCH 5 1830. BY JOHN CUMBERLAND. 8. BRECKNOCK PLACE. CAMDEN TOWN.

Selected Bibliography

The following sources have been especially useful in my study of Dickens and *Little Dorrit*.

Auerbach, Erich. *Mimesis: The Representation of Reality in Western Literature.* Trans. Willard R. Trask. Princeton: Princeton UP, 1953.

Barickman, Richard. The Spiritual Journey of Amy Dorrit and Arthur Clennam: "A Way Wherein There Is No Ecstasy." *Dickens Studies Annual.* Ed. Robert B. Partlow, Jr. Carbondale: Southern Illinois UP, 1978. 7, 163–89.

Brown, Arthur Washburn. *Sexual Analysis of Dickens' Props.* New York: Emerson, 1971.

Burgan, William. "People in the Setting of *Little Dorrit.*" *Texas Studies in Literature and Language.* Austin: Univ. of Texas. 15 (Spring 1973), 1, 111–28.

Carlisle, Janice. M. "*Little Dorrit*: Necessary Fictions." *Studies in the Novel.* Ed. James W. Lee. Denton: North State UP, 1975. 7, 195–214.

———. *The Sense of an Audience: Dickens, Thackery and George Eliot at Mid-Century.* Athens: Univ. of Georgia Press, 1981.

Charles Dickens' Uncollected Writings from Household Words: 1850–1859. Ed. Harry Stone. 2 vols. Bloomington: Indiana UP, 1968.

Christmas, Peter. "*Little Dorrit*: The End of Good and Evil." *Dickens Studies Annual.* Carbondale: Southern Illinois UP, 1977. 6, 134–53.

Collins, Philip. *Dickens and Crime.* Bloomington: Indiana UP, 1962.

Davis, Paul B. "Dickens, Hogarth and the Illustrated *Great Expectations.*" *Dickensian*, 80 (1984) 130–143.

Dickens: The Critical Heritage. Ed. Philip Collins. New York: Barnes and Noble, 1971.

Dunn, Richard J. "David Copperfield's Carlylean Retailoring." *Dickens the Craftsman: Strategies of Presentation.* Carbondale: Southern Illinois UP, 1970, pp. 95–114.

Dyson, A.E. *The Inimitable Dickens.* London: Macmillan, 1970.

Easson, Angus. "Marshalsea Prisoners: Mr. Dorrit and Mr. Hemens." *Dickens Studies Annual.* Ed. Robert B. Partlow, Jr. Carbondale: Southern Illinois UP, 1972. 3, 77–86.

Emery, John Pike. *Arthur Murphy: An Eminent English Dramatist of the Eighteenth Century*. Philadelphia: Univ. of Pennsylvania Press, 1946.

Forsyth, William. 'Literary Style.' *Fraser's*. 55 (March 1857), 260–3.

Galt, John. *The Lives of the Players*. London: Colburn and Bentley, 1831. Vol. II.

Graver, Suzanne. "Writing in a 'Womanly' Way and the Double Vision of *Bleak House*." *Dickens Quarterly*. Ed. David Paroissien. Carbondale: Southern Illinois UP, 4 (1987), 3–15.

Hamilton, Morse. "Nature and the Unnatural in *Little Dorrit*." *Victorians Institute Journal*. Ed. Conrad Festa. Norfolk: Old Dominion UP, 1977. 6, 9–19.

Hardy, Barbara. "The Complexity of Dickens." *Dickens 1970: Centenary Essays*. Ed. Michael Slater. London: Chapman and Hall, 1970. pp. 29–51.

House, Humphrey. *The Dickens World*. 2nd ed., 1941; rpt. Oxford: Oxford UP, 1965.

Household Words: A Weekly Journal. Ed. Charles Dickens. London: Bradbury and Evans, 1854.

Hutter, Albert D. "Reconstructive Autobiography: The Experience at Warren's Blacking." *Dickens Studies Annual*. Ed. Robert B. Partlow, Jr. Carbondale: Southern Illinois UP, 1977. 6, 1–14.

Jeaffreson, John Cordy. "Charles Dickens." *Novels and Novelists: from Elizabeth to Victoria*. London: Hurst and Blackett, 1858.

Johnson, Edgar. *Charles Dickens: His Tragedy and Triumph*. 2 vols. New York: Simon and Schuster, 1952.

Lang, Andrew, introd. *Little Dorrit*. By Charles Dickens. Gads Hill Ed. London: Chapman and Hall, 1897. pp. i–xii.

Leacock, Stephen. *Charles Dickens: His Life and Work*. New York: Doubleday, 1934.

Leavis, F.R. and Q.D. Leavis. *Dickens The Novelist*. London: Chatto and Windus, 1970.

The Letters of Charles Dickens. Eds. Georgina Hogarth and Maime Dickens. London: Chapman and Hall, 1882.

Librach, Ronald S. "The Burdens of Self and Society: Release and Redemption in *Little Dorrit*." *Studies in the Novel*. Ed. Gerald A. Kirk. Denton: North Texas State Univ., 1975. 7, 4, 538–51.

'Literary Style.' *Fraser's*. 60 (June 1857), 249–64.

"Little Dorrit." *Athenaeum*. 1 Dec. 1855, pp. 1393–5.

"Little Dorrit." *Athenaeum*. 6 June 1857, pp. 722–4.

MacKenzie, Norman and Jeanne MacKenzie. *Dickens: A Life*. Oxford: Oxford UP, 1979.

Marcus, Steven. *Dickens From Pickwick to Dombey*. New York: Basic, 1965.

Miller, J. Hillis. *Charles Dickens: The World of His Novels*. Bloomington: Indiana UP, 1958.

Monod, Sylvere. *Dickens the Novelist*. 1953; rpt. Norman: Univ. of Oklahoma Press, 1968.

Mr. and Mrs. Charles Dickens: His Letters to Her. Ed. Walter Dexter. New York: Haskell, 1972.

Nadel, Ira Bruce. 'Wonderful Deception': Art and the Artist in *Little Dorrit*. *Criticism*. Detroit: Wayne State, 1977. 19, 17–33.

Romano, John. *Dickens and Reality*. New York: Columbia UP, 1978.

Roopnaraine, R. Rupert. "Time and the Circle in *Little Dorrit*." *Dickens Studies Annual*. Ed. Robert B. Partlow, Jr. Carbondale: Southern Illinois UP, 1972. 3, 54–76.

Rosenberg, Brian. "The Language of Doubt in *Oliver Twist*." *Dickens Quarterly*. Ed. David Paroissien. Carbondale: Southern Illinois UP, 1987. 4, 2, 91–8.

Slater, Michael. "Dickens." *The English Novel: Select Bibliographical Guides*. Ed. A.E. Dyson. Oxford: Oxford UP, 1974.

———. *Dickens and Women*. Stanford: Stanford, UP, 1983.

Slochower, Harry. *Mythopoesis: Mythic Patterns in the Literary Classics*. Detroit: Wayne State UP, 1970.

Splitter, Randolph. "Guilt and the Trappings of Melodrama in *Little Dorrit*." *Dickens Studies Annual*. Ed. Robert B. Partlow, Jr. Carbondale: Southern Illinois UP, 1977. 6, 119–33.

Stang, Richard. "*Little Dorrit*: A World in Reverse." *Dickens the Craftsman: Strategies of Presentation*. Carbondale: Southern Illinois UP, 1970. pp. 140–64.

Stephen, James Fitzjames. "Little Dorrit." *Saturday Review*. 4 July 1857, 4, 15.

Stone, Harry. "The Love Pattern in Dickens' Novels." *Dickens the Craftsman: Strategies of Presentation*. Carbondale: Southern Illinois Univ. Press, 1970, pp. 1–20.

Stonehouse, John Harrison. *Green Leaves: New Chapters in the Life of Charles Dickens*. London: Sotheran, 1931.

Storey, Gladys. *Dickens and Daughter*. London: Muller, 1939.

Sucksmith, Harvey Peter. *The Narrative Art of Charles Dickens: The Rhetoric of Sympathy and Irony in His Novels*. Oxford: Clarendon, 1970.

Surveyor, Edouard Fabre. *Dickens in France*. London: Dickens Fellowship, 1932.

Taine, Hippolyte. *The History of English Literature*. 1872; rpt. New York: Unger, 1965.

Tick, Stanley. "The Sad End of Mr. Meagles." *Dickens Studies Annual*. Ed. Robert B. Partlow, Jr. Carbondale: Southern Illinois Univ. Press, 1972. 3, 87–99.

Tillotston, Kathleen. *Novels of the Eighteen-Forties*. London: Clarendon, 1954.

Trilling, Lionel. "Freud and Literature." *Psychoanalysis and Literature*. Ed. Hendrik M. Ruitenbeek. New York: Dutton, 1964, pp. 251–71.

————. *The Opposing Self*. New York: Harcourt, 1955.

Watt, Ian. *The Rise of the Novel*. Berkeley: Univ. of California Press, 1957.

Webb, R. K. "The Victorian Reading Public." *The Pelican Guide to English Literature: From Dickens to Hardy*. Ed. Boris Ford. Baltimore: Penguin, 1958, pp. 205–26.

Weiser, Irwin. "Reformed But Unrewarded: Pip's Progress." *Dickens Studies Newsletter*. Ed. David Paroissien. 4 (1983), 143–5.

Widdows, Margharita. *English Literature*. London: Chatto and Windus, 1928.

Wilde, Alan. "Mr. F.'s Aunt and the Analogical Structure of 'Little Dorrit.' " *Nineteenth Century Fiction*. Los Angeles: Univ. of California Press, 1964–5. 19, 33–44.

Wilson, Angus. "Dickens on Children and Childhood." *Dickens 1970: Centenary Essays*. Ed. Michael Slater. London: Chapman and Hall, 1970, pp. 195–227.

Wilson, Edmund. *A Literary Chronicle: 1920–1950*. New York: Doubleday, 1956.

————. *The Wound and the Bow*. New York: Oxford Univ. Press, 1947.

Wing, George. "Mr. F.'s Aunt: A Laughing Matter." *English Studies in Canada*. Frederikstown: Univ. of New Brunswick Press, 1977. 3, 207–15.

————. "Patterns of Criticism." *Dickens*. Edinburgh: Oliver and Boyd, 1966, pp. 88–105.

Woodward, Kathleen. "Passivity and Passion in *Little Dorrit*." *Dickensian*. Ed. Michael Slater. London: Dickens Fellowship, 1975. 71, 3, 140–48.

Young, Melanie. "Distorted Expectations: Pip and the Problems of Language." *Dickens Studies Annual*. Ed. Robert B. Partlow, Jr. Carbondale: Southern Illinois Univ. Press, 1978. 7, 203–220.

Zimmerman, James R. "Sun and Shadow in *Little Dorrit*." *Dickensian*. 83 (1987), 93–105.

Index

Steven E. Alford

IRONY AND THE LOGIC OF THE ROMANTIC IMAGINATION

American University Studies: Series III (Comparative Literature). Vol. 13
ISBN 0-8204-0110-2   184 pages   paperback US $ 19.45

Recommended price – alterations reserved

This study examines romantic irony as a principle of style in the work of Friedrich Schlegel and William Blake. The first half traces Schlegel's critique of the principles of identity and noncontradiction, his development of a *romantic logic*, his view of dialectic and rhetoric, and how romantic irony is a stylistic mirror of the results of his critique of formal logic. These findings are tested in a close reading of his essay *Über die Unverständlichkeit* (1800). The second part examines the suggestive relation between Blake and Schlegel's views on logic, dialectic, and rhetoric, and uses these views as the basis for a reading of *The Marriage of Heaven and Hell* (1794). Both thinkers support the conclusion that romantic irony as a principle of style has two moments which can be characterized hermeneutically as negative dialectical and performative.

Contents: This study examines romantic irony as a principle of style in the work of Friedrich Schlegel and William Blake, using Schlegel's «Über die Unverständlichkeit» and Blake's «The Marriage of Heaven and Hell.»

PETER LANG PUBLISHING, INC.
62 West 45th Street
USA – New York, NY 10036

John W. Crawford

EARLY SHAKESPEAREAN ACTRESSES

American University Studies: Series IV (English Language and Literature).
Vol. 8
ISBN 0-8204-0099-8   205 pages   hardback US $ 25.00*

*Recommended price – alterations reserved

One of the innovations of the Restoration in England was to introduce publicly the female actor on stage, with the reopening of the theatres. Charles II not only created two companies with this return to England, but promoted the concept of females as actors. It took courage for the first ones to enter this questionable vocation, considering the history the stage had achieved in Elizabethan and Stuart times, a history that demonstrated much criticism about the morality of dramatists and actors. Restoration actresses like George Anne Bellamy and Dora Jordan, as well as early eighteenth-century actresses like Catherine Clive and Peg Woffington proved that much individuality did indeed exist among the first; and even though the theatre had gained a much better reputation by the early nineteenth century, still actresses like Ellen Terry and Julia Marlowe were often the talk of the town because of their personal lives. Yet, these women proved that there is a place for the actress in modern drama.

Contents: 1. Brief background of the world of actors of the sixteenth century – 2. Individual sketches of various early actresses of Shakespearean roles – 2. Summary essay of certain actresses and their influence on Shakespearean drama.

PETER LANG PUBLISHING, INC.
62 West 45th Street
USA – New York, NY 10036

Alexander Weiss

CHAUCER'S NATIVE HERITAGE

American University Studies: Series IV (English Language and Literature).
Vol. 11
ISBN 0-8204-0128-5   257 pages   hardcover/lam. US $ 29.25

Recommended price – alterations reserved

Although much scholarly inquiry has been devoted to identifying foreign influences on Chaucer's poetry, perhaps its single most commonly acknowledged quality, and one for which it has been universally praised, is its «Englishness». *Chaucer's Native Heritage* is an attempt to isolate and define this English quality; to demonstrate that it has its roots in earlier English poetry, particularly in the early Middle English lyrics, and, consequently, that Chaucer's poetry does not so much represent the beginning of a new tradition in English literature as the culmination of a native poetic tradition to which he was heir.

Contents: Review of scholarship examining Chaucer's indebtedness to native influence; continuity of English poetic tradition; medieval English and continental lyric poetry; Chaucer's «Englishness» and its sources in native poetic tradition.

PETER LANG PUBLISHING, INC.
62 West 45th Street
USA – New York, NY 10036